SPIRITUAL

STORIES

AS TOLD BY

RAMANA MAHARSHI

D1104650

SRI RAMANASRAMAM

TIRUVANNAMALAI

2006

© Sri Ramanasramam
Tiruvannamalai

Fifth edition 1999 - 1000 copies
Sixth (revised) edition 2001 - 2000 copies
Seventh edition 2002 - 2000 copies
Eighth edition 2004 - 3000 copies
Ninth edition 2006 - 3000 copies

CC No: 1058

ISBN: 81-88018-35-X

Price: Rs. Rs.40/-

Published by
V. S. RAMANAN
President, Board of Trustees
SRI RAMANASRAMAM
Tiruvannamalai 606 603
S. India

Typeset at:
Sri Ramanasramam

Offset by:
Sudarsan Graphics
Chennai - 600 017

PREFACE

The mind seeks to define the infinite. In doing so it has used its own resources to bring down Supreme Truth in a simple and yet potent language. Scattered throughout the religious scriptures of India, parables and stories abound, weaving a colourful thread around the most profound spiritual truths of mankind. Handed down from parent to child these religious treasures of India remain a relevant force today.

Sivaprakasam Pillai, one of the earliest devotees to recognise the spiritual greatness of Bhagavan Sri Ramana Maharshi, commented "Sri Ramana Bhagavan has attained the state of *Brahman* without knowing the word *Brahman.*" For it was not until years later, that books were brought to Sri Bhagavan by devotees, describing the very state he himself had intuitively experienced. With his pure and retentive memory, he retained the essence of all these books at a glance, and brought forth at a moment's notice, the perfect story or parable suitable to the occasion. In Sri Ramana's own words the beauty and wisdom contained in such stories are made ever more beautiful and the essence made even clearer.

Sri Bhagavan would not only tell the story but would act out the part to the delight of his devotees. If the story was particularly moving, tears would flow freely from his eyes. "Such was the attraction of these stories", Kunju Swami related, "that when we heard Sri Bhagavan beginning a story, even if we had heard it numerous times before, we would literally stop whatever we were doing and run to his side to hear it again!" S. S. Cohen in *Guru Ramana* relates, "Bhagavan was reciting from memory a poem of a Vaishnava Saint, in which occurred the words, 'Fold me in Thy embrace, O Lord', whereupon the arms of

Bhagavan joined in a circle round the vacant air in front of him, while his eyes shone with devotional fervour and his voice shook with stifled sobs which did not escape our notice. It was fascinating to see him acting the parts he related, and being in such exhilarated moods as these." On another occasion while Bhagavan was reading and explaining a story about *Tara Vilasam* his eyes became full of tears and his voice became tremulous. It looked as if the whole drama was being enacted in his presence. Noticing this Suri Nagamma remarked, "Bhagavan appears to have been transformed into Tara herself." Pulling himself together the master said with a smile, "What to do? I identify myself with whosoever is before me, I have no separate identity. I am universal."

At the suggestion of Mrs. Lucia Osborne, we have included the incidents which inspired Sri Bhagavan to relate the story. A few new stories have been added, along with a glossary of Sanskrit and Tamil words. Special thanks must be made to Sri S. Tyagarajan who with great care went over the entire manuscript with Sri Kunju Swamigal. Sri Kunju Swamigal's unfailing enthusiasm and keen interest helped us greatly.

With deepest salutations this little work is offered to Sri Bhagavan, whose guidance, grace and love has prompted this collection of stories. We pray for the grace and blessings of Bhagavan Sri Ramana. May his words inspire us to turn within.

Sri Ramanasramam   Joan Greenblatt
August 5, 1984

FOREWORD

Everyone knows that Sri Bhagavan Ramana was a master story teller! Sri Ramanasramam publications, like *Letters, Day by Day*, and *Talks*, abound with marvellous accounts of how Bhagavan picturesquely narrated, rather enacted, incidents that took place in the lives of sages and saints and traditional stories of great spiritual content, like the story of Sage Ribhu.

Seeing how the first edition of this book was serving devotees, the compiler, Mrs. Joan Greenblatt, worked one-pointed to enlarge and improve it; the result is the excellent second edition now in your hand!

We hope all seekers will find this book both interesting and enlightening and partake of the Spiritual Presence which lies within its pages and the abundant grace of the narrator Sri Ramana Himself!

Sri Ramanasramam
Maha Sivarathri
17.2.85

Sri T. N. Venkataraman
President, Board of Trustees

CONTENTS

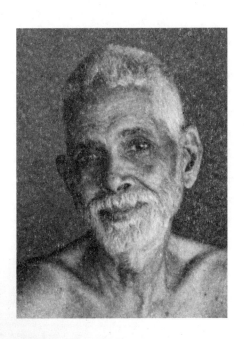

Various Stories & Tales

Sri Bhagavan became transformed while relating incidents from his vast collection of stories and tales. On one occasion while describing Gautama's joy at Goddess Parvati's coming to his Ashram, Sri Bhagavan could not go on, for tears filled his eyes and emotion choked his voice. Trying to hide his plight from others, he remarked, "I don't know how people who perform *Harikatha* explain such passages to audiences and manage to do it without breaking down. I suppose they must make their hearts hard like stone before starting their work."

SELF-SURRENDER

D: I fear that Self-realisation is no easy thing to attain.
M: Why impede yourself by anticipating failure? Push
on. Self-realisation will come to an earnest seeker in a trice.
To illustrate this, Sri Bhagavan told the following story:

KING JANAKA WAS listening to a philosophical treatise read
by the state pandit, wherein a passage occurred to the effect that
a rider who had placed one foot in the stirrup, contemplating
upon realisation could realise the Self before he lifted the other
foot to place it in the other stirrup. That is, the passage taught,
that when realisation comes, it comes in an instant. The king
stopped the pandit from proceeding further, and ordered him
to prove the statement. The pandit admitted that he was only a
book-worm and was unable to impart practical wisdom. Janaka
suggested that the text was either false or exaggerated, but the
pandit would not agree to this. Though he himself was unable
to impart practical wisdom, he maintained that the text could
not be false or exaggerated, since it contained the words of wise
sages of the past. Janaka was annoyed with the pandit and in a
fit of rage condemned him to prison. He then inflicted the
same punishment on every pandit who passed for a wise man
but was unable to prove this scriptural text.

For fear of being imprisoned, some of the pandits fled the
country in voluntary exile. While two or three of them were running
through a thick forest, a sage called Ashtavakra,* who though young

---

* *Ashta* means 'eight' and *vakra* means 'bends'. Ashtavakra was so named
because his body had eight deformities.

3

in age was wise in learning, happened to cross their path. Having learnt their plight, Ashtavakra offered to prove the text true to the king and thereby have the imprisoned pandits released. Impressed by his bold assurance, they took him in a palanquin to the king. At the sight of the sage, the king stood up and saluted him with great reverence. Ashtavakra then ordered the king to release all the pandits. Janaka thought that such an order could come only from one who had the capacity to set his doubts at rest, and hence he released all the pandits and asked the sage whether he could summon the horse. The sage advised him not to be in a hurry and suggested that they should go to a solitary spot. Thereupon the king on his horse and the sage in a palanquin went out of the city towards the forest. When they reached the forest the sage asked the king to send back the retinue. The king did as he was asked, and then placing one of his feet in the stirrup, he requested the sage to prove the scriptural text. But the sage replied by asking whether the position in which they stood indicated a proper master-disciple relationship. The king then understood that he should show due reverence towards Ashtavakra, and prayed to him for grace. The sage then addressed him as 'Janaka', since he was no longer a king and told him that before being taught *Brahma jnana*, a true disciple should surrender himself and all his possessions to his Master. "So be it", said the king. "So be it" replied the sage and disappeared into the forest. From that moment Janaka stood transfixed with one foot in the stirrup and the other dangling in the air, as if he were a statue. (Saying this, Sri Bhagavan imitated the posture of King Janaka).

Time passed by, and the citizens, finding no sign of their king returning, grew anxious and began to search for him. They came to the place where Janaka was standing transfixed and were dismayed to find him unaware of their presence and indifferent to their earnest enquiries. They therefore began searching for Ashtavakra who, they thought, must be a charlatan that had cast a spell upon their king, and vowed vengeance upon him. At the same time, being concerned with the king's condition and wanting to minister to him, they brought him back to the city on a palanquin. The king, however, continued to remain in the same condition.

At last, having found Ashtavakra, the ministers entreated him to remove the alleged spell and bring the king back to his normal condition. At the same time they charged him with the responsibility for having cast the spell. Ashtavakra treated their ignorant remarks with contempt and called the name of Janaka, who immediately saluted him, and responded to his call. The ministers were surprised. Ashtavakra told the king that he was being maliciously accused by the people of having brought him to some sad plight and asked him to tell the truth. On hearing this, the king angrily asked, 'Who said so'? The ministers were taken by surprise and pleaded for mercy. Thereupon, the sage advised the king to resume his normal functions, adding that *Brahma jnana* could be taught only to competent persons and that since the king had successfully passed the test, he would now impart it to him. Then the sage remained alone with the king during the night and taught him the ultimate Truth, saying "*Brahman* is not anything new or apart from oneself and no particular time or place is needed to realise It." He finally concluded by saying, "That Thou Art" (*tat tvam asi*). That is the Self, eternal and infinite.

The next morning the ministers found that the king called the assembly and performed his functions as usual. In the assembled court Ashtavakra asked the king whether his former doubt about whether *Brahma jnana* could be attained as suddenly and as quickly as mentioned in the scriptures was cleared, and if so to bring the horse and demonstrate the truth of it.

The king was all humility now and said, "Lord! Because of my immaturity, I doubted the correctness of the scriptural text. I now realise every letter of it is true." The ministers thanked the sage.

5

THE *JNANI* AND THE *SIDDHA*

One day, while speaking about hatha yoga *and related subjects, Sri Bhagavan narrated the following story from* Prabhulingalila, *a well-known Tamil work by the Sage Sivaprakasa Swamigal.*

PRABHULINGA, THE FOUNDER of the Lingayat sect (now mostly prevalent in Karnataka State only), was touring the land for the uplift of the spiritually minded. He met the famous Yogi Gorakhnath in Gokarnam (a famous place of Hindu pilgrimage on the west coast of India). The yogi welcomed him respectfully, but was however, proudly conscious of his own extraordinary powers over the elements. He considered his guest more or less his equal, expressed pleasure at meeting him, and upon greeting him, asked who he was.

Prabhulinga replied that only the One who had destroyed his ego, root and branch, and who had thereby realised himself could know who he was, and wondered what he could say to a non-entity, a person, who clung to his perishable body.

Gorakhnath, who identified his body as himself, replied, "That person alone who has gained the immortality of the body, by the favour of Siva and consumption of *gulikas* (medicinal herbs), will never die. Therefore one who had not gained such immortality dies."

Prabhulinga remarked that knowledge consists in realizing one's Self and not in immortalising the body and went on to explain at length that the body cannot be the real Self. However, Gorakhnath could not be persuaded and would not budge an inch from his ground; he proudly challenged Prabhulinga to try cutting his body, handing him a long, bright and sharp sword. When the sword struck the body of Gorakhnath, it caused him no injury but was itself blunted. Prabhulinga feigned surprise, and asked Gorakhnath to try cutting his body. At first Gorakhnath hesitated to do so saying that Prabhulinga would die. But when Prabhulinga insisted, he took up the sword and tried to cut his body. To the great surprise of Gorakhnath, the sword passed easily through the body of Prabhulinga without affecting it in any way. It was as if the sword was passing through empty space! Only then was Gorakhnath, the *Siddha*, ready to acknowledge the superiority of Prabhulinga, the *Jnani*. Thus his pride was humbled, and he prayed to Prabhulinga, to teach him the truth. Prabhulinga then expounded *Brahma vidya* to Gorakhnath as follows: "Gorakhnath, do not think your body to be your Self. Seek the In-dweller (the cave-dweller) and you will once for all rid yourself of the disease of birth and death. The cave is your heart only, the In-dweller thereof is called God and I am That."

TWENTYFOUR GURUS

A KING WAS passing through a forest in all pomp and pageantry, with his army and retinue behind him. He came across a man with not even a cod-piece on, lying on the ground, with one leg cocked over the other. He was laughing away, apparently supremely happy, contented with himself and all the world. The king was struck with the man's happy state and sent for him. But when the king's men approached the nude ascetic and delivered the king's message, he took absolutely no notice and continued in his ascetic bliss. On being told of this, the king himself went to the man and even then the man took no notice. Thereupon it struck the king that this must be no common man, and said, 'Swami, you are evidently supremely happy. May we know what is the secret of such happiness and from which guru you learnt it?' Thereupon the ascetic told the king, 'I have had twentyfour gurus. Everything, this body, the earth, the birds, some instruments, some persons, all have taught me'. All the things in the world may be classed as either good or bad. The good taught him what he must seek. Similarly, the bad taught him what he must avoid. The ascetic was Dattatreya, the *avadhuta*.

ENTER THE HEART

A devotee who had suddenly lost his only son came to Bhagavan in a state of acute grief, seeking relief. He asked a few questions in which his grief was evident. Bhagavan, as usual, asked him to enquire into the Self and find out who is grieving. The devotee was not satisfied. Bhagavan then said, "All right. I will tell you a story from Vichara Sagaram. *Listen".*

TWO YOUNGSTERS BY name Rama and Krishna, told their respective parents that they would go to foreign countries to prosecute further studies and then earn a lot of money. After some time, one of them died suddenly. The other studied well, earned a lot and was living happily. Some time later the one that was alive requested a merchant who was going to his native place to tell his father that he was wealthy and happy and that the other boy who had come with him had passed away. Instead of passing on the information correctly, the merchant told the father of the person who was alive, that his son was dead, and the father of the person that was dead, that his son had earned a lot of money and was living happily. The parents of the person that was actually dead, were happy in the thought that their son would come back after some time, while the parents of the person whose son was alive, but was reported to be dead, were in great grief. In fact, neither of them saw their son but they were experiencing happiness or grief according to the reports they received. That is all. We too are similarly situated. We believe all sorts of things that the mind tells us and get deluded into thinking that what exists does not exist and that what does not exist exists. If we do not believe the mind but enter the heart and see the son that is inside, there is no need to see the children outside.

BUDDHA

During a conversation on non-attachment, Bhagavan said, "In this part of the country, one of our ancients wrote, 'O Lord, thou hast given me a hand to use as pillow under my head, a cloth to cover my loins, hands wherewith to eat food, what more do I want? This is my great good fortune'! That is the purport of the verse. Is it really possible to say how great a good fortune that is? Even the greatest kings wish for such happiness. There is nothing to equal it. Having experienced both these conditions, I know the difference between this and that. These beds, sofa and articles around me – all this is bondage."

"Is not the Buddha an example of this?" asked a devotee. Thereupon Sri Bhagavan began speaking about Buddha.

"YES," SAID BHAGAVAN, "when the Buddha was in the palace with all possible luxuries in the world, he was still sad. To remove his sadness, his father created more luxuries than ever. But none of them satisfied the Buddha. At midnight he left his wife and child and disappeared. He remained in great austerity for six years, realised the Self; and for the welfare of the world became a mendicant (*bhikshu*). It was only after he became a mendicant that he enjoyed great bliss. Really, what more did he require?"

"In the garb of a mendicant he came to his own city, did he not?" asked a devotee.

"Yes, yes," said Bhagavan. "Having heard that he was coming, his father, Suddhodana, decorated the royal elephant

10

and went out with his whole army to receive him on the main road. But without touching the main road, the Buddha came by side roads and by-lanes; he sent his close associates to the various streets for alms while he himself in the guise of a mendicant went by another way to his father. How could the father know that his son was coming in that guise! Yasodhara (the Buddha's wife), however, recognised him, made her son prostrate before his father and herself prostrated. After that, the father recognised the Buddha. Suddhodana however, had never expected to see his son in such a state and was very angry and shouted, 'Shame on you! What is this garb? Does one who should have the greatest of riches come like this? I've had enough of it!' And with that, he looked furiously at the Buddha. Regretting that his father had not yet got rid of his ignorance, the Buddha too, began to look at his father with even greater intensity. In this war of looks, the father was defeated. He fell at the feet of his son and himself became a mendicant. Only a man with non-attachment can know the power of non-attachment", said Bhagavan, his voice quivering with emotion.

The *Sadhu* and the
Three Stones

*In 1949 the inauguration of Mother's Temple took place,
and the dedicated labour of ten years was consecrated in Sri
Bhagavan's presence. In front of the Matrubhuteswara Shrine,
the Jubilee Hall was built to accommodate the ever-increasing
number of devotees. A large granite couch was installed with
elaborate carvings, spread with a silken mattress for Bhagavan's
comfort. As a big pillow was placed on one side for Bhagavan to
keep his arms, another behind him to lean against and a third
one at his feet, the actual seating space was considerably reduced.
One day when Suri Nagamma entered the hall Sri Bhagavan
said, looking at his attendants, "See how this mattress slips from
one side to another! People think that it will be comfortable for
Bhagavan if there is a costly mattress. It is, however, not possible
to sit on this restfully. Why this? It would be much more
comfortable if I sat on the stone seat itself. As told in the story
about the* sadhu, *people think that Swami is undergoing great
hardship when he lives in a thatched shed and lies on a stone
bench, and so they make a fuss. It will perhaps be better if, like
that* sadhu *in the story, I gather some stones similar to those I
had in the Virupaksha Cave, take them to whichever place I
go, and spread them on a mattress like this."*

A devotee asked, "What is that story of the sadhu *which
Bhagavan has now mentioned?" Whereupon Bhagavan
began relating the following story.*

A GREAT MAHATMA was living as a *sadhu* under a tree in a
forest. He always used to keep with him three stones. While

12

sleeping, he used to keep one of them under the head, another under the waist and the third under the legs and cover himself with a sheet. When it rained, the body used to be on the stones and so the water would flow underneath, and the water that fell on the sheet too, would flow down. So there was no disturbance to his sleep; he used to sleep soundly. When sitting, he used to keep the three stones together like a hearth and sit upon them comfortably. Hence snakes and other reptiles did not trouble him nor did he trouble them, for they used to crawl through the slits under the stones. Somebody used to bring him food and he would eat it. And so, there was nothing for him to worry about.

A king, who came to that forest for hunting, saw this *sadhu* and felt, 'What a pity! How much must he be suffering by having to adjust his body suitably to those stones and sleep thereon. I will take him home and keep him with me for at least one or two days and make him feel comfortable'. So thinking, he went home and sent two of his soldiers with a palanquin and bearers, with instructions to invite the *sadhu* respectfully and bring him to his palace. He also said that if they did not succeed in bringing the *sadhu*, they would be punished. They came and saw the *sadhu* and told him that the king had ordered them to bring him to the palace and that he should come. When he showed disinclination to go with them, they said that they would be punished if they returned without him. So they begged of him to come, if only to save them from trouble. As he did not want them to get into trouble on his account, he agreed to go with them. What was there for him to pack up? A *kaupeenam*, a sheet and those three stones. He folded and kept the *kaupeenam* in that sheet, kept those three stones also in the sheet and tied them together. 'What is this? This Swami is bringing with him some stones when he is going to a Raja's palace! Is he mad or what?' thought those soldiers. Anyway, he got into the palanquin with his bundle and came to the king. The Raja saw the bundle, and thinking it contained some personal effects, took him into the palace with due respect, feasted him properly and arranged a tape cot with a mattress of silk cotton to sleep upon. The *sadhu* opened his bundle, took out the three stones, spread them on the bed, covered himself with the sheet and slept as usual.

The next morning the king came, bowed to him with respect and asked, "Swami, is it comfortable for you here?"

Swami: "Yes. What is there wanting here? I am always happy."

King: "That is not it, Swami. You were experiencing hardships in the forest by having to sleep on those stones. Here this bed and this house must be giving you happiness. That is why I am asking."

Swami: "The bed that was there is here also. The bed that is here is there also. So I have the same happiness everywhere. There is nothing wanting at any time, either in regard to my sleep or to my happiness."

The king was puzzled and looked at the cot. He saw that the three stones were on it. Whereupon, the king immediately prostrated himself before the *sadhu* and said, "Oh great man! Without knowing your greatness I brought you here with the intention of making you happy. I did not know that you are always in a state of happiness, and so I behaved in this foolish manner. Please excuse me and bless me." After making up for his mistake in this way, he allowed the *sadhu* to go his way. This is the story of the *sadhu*.

"So, in the eyes of Mahatmas, the free life is the real happy life?" asked that devotee. "What else? Life in big buildings like this is like prison life. Only I may be an 'A' class prisoner. When I sit on mattresses like these, I feel that I am sitting on prickly pears. Where is peace and comfort?" said Bhagavan.

Next day that mattress was taken away and the usual mattress was spread on the couch. Even so, several people thought that it might be better to leave Bhagavan to a free life like that of the *sadhu*. But Bhagavan had to stay there alone, like a parrot in the cage of the devotees, because the devotees never leave him free.

14

INITIATION

A devotee asked, "Can anyone get any benefit by repeating sacred syllables (mantras) picked up casually?"

Sri Bhagavan replied, "No. He must be competent and initiated in such mantras." To illustrate this he told the following story.

A KING VISITED his minister in his residence. There he was told that the minister was engaged in repetition of sacred syllables (*japa*). The king waited for him and, on meeting him, asked what the *japa* was. The minister said that it was the holiest of all, *Gayatri*. The king desired to be initiated by the minister but the minister confessed his inability to initiate him. Therefore the king learned it from someone else, and meeting the minister later he repeated the *Gayatri* and wanted to know if it was right. The minister said that the *mantra* was correct, but it was not proper for him to say it. When pressed for an explanation the minister called to a page close by and ordered him to take hold of the king. The order was not obeyed. The order was often repeated, and still not obeyed. The king flew into a rage and ordered the same man to hold the minister, and it was immediately done. The minister laughed and said that the incident was the explanation required by the king. "How?" asked the king. The minister replied, "The order was the same and the executor also, but the authority was different. When I ordered, the effect was *nil* whereas, when you ordered, there was immediate effect. Similarly with *mantras*."

PEACE IS THE SOLE CRITERION

When asked about the characteristics of a jnani, Bhagavan said, "They are described in books, such as the Bhagavad Gita, but we must bear in mind that the jnani's state is one which transcends the mind. It cannot be described by the mind. Only Silence can correctly describe this state and its characteristics. Silence is more effective than speech. From Silence came the ego, from the ego came thought, and from thought came speech. So if speech is effective, how much more effective must be its original source!" Then, in this connection Sri Bhagavan related the following story.

TATTVARAYA COMPOSED A *bharani* (a kind of poetic composition in Tamil) in honour of his Guru Swarupananda and convened an assembly of learned *pandits* to hear the work and assess its value. The *pandits* raised the objection that a *bharani* was only composed in honour of great heroes capable of killing a thousand elephants, and that it was not in order to compose such a work in honour of an ascetic. Thereupon the author said, "Let us all go to my guru and we shall have this matter settled there." They went to the guru and, after all had taken their seats, the author told his guru the purpose of their coming there. The guru sat silent and all the others also remained in *mauna*. The whole day passed, night came, and some more days and nights, and yet all sat there silently, no thought at all occurring to any of them and nobody asked why they had come there. After three or four days like this, the guru moved his mind a bit, and thereupon the assembly regained their thought activity. They then declared, "Conquering a thousand elephants is nothing compared to the guru's power to conquer the rutting elephants of all our egos put together. So certainly he deserves the *bharani* in his honour!"

THE GARLIC PLANT

While Bhagavan was perusing the monthly journal Grihalakshmi *he began to laugh and handed the journal to Suri Nagamma as she was leaving the hall, saying, "The greatness of garlic is described in it. Please read it." The article contained recipes for making* chutneys *and pickles and in conclusion it stated that there is nothing equal to it in its greatness and its benefit to the body. When Suri Nagamma returned to the hall in the afternoon, Sri Bhagavan inquired if she had read the article and said, "People say it is very good for health. Really it is so. It cures rheumatism and gives strength to the body. For children it acts like* amrit *(nectar). Garlic is also known as* amrit."

A devotee asked how it got that name. Sri Bhagavan replied, "There is a curious story about it," and began telling the following story.

AS IS WELL known, when gods (*devas*) and demons (*rakshasas*) churned the ocean, *amrit* came out of it. When the *rakshasas* were running away with the vessel containing *amrit*, the *devas* appealed to Vishnu. Vishnu came on to the scene in the shape of Mohini (enchantress), and offered to resolve their quarrel by serving *amrit* to them all. They agreed. While serving it to the gods first, it appeared that there might not be enough to go round for the demons. One of the latter got into the line of the gods, unobserved by Mohini, and was swallowing the *amrit*, when the Sun and Moon noticed it and gave her the hint. She threw the ladle, with which the *amrit* was being served, at the demon in such a way as to cut off his head. The ladle became the *Chakra* (an invincible lethal weapon of Vishnu) and cut off his head. But as the *amrit* had already gone down his throat, the head became a *graha* (planet) and has since been taking vengeance on the Sun and Moon at the time of an eclipse. That is the story. Now, when the head of the demon was severed, the trunk fell down, and in the process, a few drops of *amrit* fell on the ground. It is said that those drops became the garlic plant. That is why it is said that garlic has some of the properties of *amrit*. It is very good for the body. But since it also has the touch of the demon, it has tamasic qualities too, which when eaten affect the mind. Hence, it is forbidden for *sadhakas*.

'I' AND YOU

An earnest devotee asked Sri Bhagavan about the method to realize the Self. As usual, Sri Bhagavan told him to find out who is the 'I' in his question. After a few more questions in this strain the devotee asked, "Instead of enquiring 'Who am I?', can I put the question to myself 'Who are you?' since then, my mind may be fixed on you whom I consider to be God in the form of Guru."

Sri Bhagavan replied, "Whatever form your enquiry may take, you must finally come to the one 'I', the Self. All these distinctions made between 'I' and 'you', master and disciple, are merely a sign of one's ignorance. That 'I' Supreme alone is. To think otherwise is to delude oneself." Thereupon Sri Bhagavan told the following story.

A *PURANIC* STORY of Sage Ribhu and his disciple Nidagha, is particularly instructive.

Although Ribhu taught his disciple the Supreme Truth of the One *Brahman* without a second, Nidagha, in spite of his erudition and understanding, did not get sufficient conviction to adopt and follow the path of *jnana*, but settled down in his native town to lead a life devoted to the observance of ceremonial religion.

But the sage loved his disciple as deeply as the latter venerated his Master. In spite of his age, Ribhu would himself go to his disciple in the town, just to see how far the latter had outgrown his ritualism. At times the sage went in disguise, so that he might observe how Nidagha would act when he did not know that he was being observed by his master.

On one such occasion Ribhu, who had put on the disguise of a rustic, found Nidagha intently watching a royal procession.

Unrecognised by the town-dweller Nidagha, the village rustic enquired what the bustle was all about, and was told that the king was going in procession.

"Oh! It is the king. He goes in procession! But where is he?" asked the rustic.

"There, on the elephant," said Nidagha.

"You say the king is on the elephant. Yes, I see the two," said the rustic, "But which is the king and which is the elephant?"

"What!" exclaimed Nidagha. "You see the two, but do not know that the man above is the king and the animal below is the elephant? What is the use of talking to a man like you?"

"Pray, be not impatient with an ignorant man like me," begged the rustic. "But you said 'above' and 'below' – what do they mean?"

Nidagha could stand it no more. "You see the king and the elephant, the one *above* and the other *below*. Yet you want to know what is meant by 'above' and 'below'?" burst out Nidagha. "If things seen and words spoken can convey so little to you, action alone can teach you. Bend forward, and you will know it all too well".

The rustic did as he was told. Nidagha got on his shoulders and said, "Know it now. I am *above* as the king, you are *below* as the elephant. Is that clear enough?"

"No, not yet," was the rustic's quiet reply. "You say you are above like the king, and I am below like the elephant. The 'king', the 'elephant', 'above' and 'below' – so far it is clear. But pray, tell me what you mean by '*I*' and '*you*'?"

When Nidagha was thus confronted all of a sudden with the mighty problem of defining the 'you' apart from the 'I', light dawned on his mind. At once he jumped down and fell at his Master's feet saying, "Who else but my venerable Master, Ribhu, could have thus drawn my mind from the superficialities of physical existence to the true Being of the Self? Oh! Benign Master, I crave thy blessings."

EARNESTNESS OR FAITH (SRADDHA)

A devotee obtained a copy of Sri Bhagavan's work Ulladu Narpadu (Forty Verses on Reality) *and began to write out the entire work for himself. Seeing him doing this writing with earnestness, though with a certain amount of difficulty and strain, since the devotee was not accustomed to squatting and doing continuous writing work, Bhagavan told the story of a* sannyasi *and his disciples to illustrate what is called* sraddha – *earnestness of purpose.*

THERE WAS ONCE a guru who had eight disciples. One day he instructed them all to make a copy of his teachings from a notebook he had kept. One of them, who had lived an easy-going life before renouncing the world, could not make a copy for himself. He, therefore paid a couple of rupees to a fellow disciple and requested him to make a copy for him also. The guru examined the copy books one day and, noticing two books in the same handwriting, asked the disciples for an explanation. Both the writer and the one on whose behalf it was written told the truth about it. The Master commented that, though speaking the truth was an essential quality of a spiritual aspirant, it alone would not carry one to one's goal, but that *sraddha* (earnestness of purpose) was also necessary. Since this had not been exhibited by the disciple who had entrusted his own labour to another, he was disqualified from discipleship. Referring to his making payment for the work, the guru sarcastically remarked that "Salvation" costs more than that and he was at liberty to purchase it rather than undergo training under him. So saying he dismissed that disciple.

IN THE WORLD BUT NOT OF THE WORLD

KADUVELI SIDDHAR WAS famed as a very austere hermit. He lived on the dry leaves fallen from trees. The king of the country heard of him and offered a reward to one who would prove this man's worth. A rich *dasi* agreed to do it. She began to live near the recluse and pretended to attend on him. She gently left pieces of *pappadam* along with the dry leaves picked by him. When he had eaten them she began to leave other kinds of tasty food along with the dry leaves. Eventually he took good tasty dishes supplied by her. They became intimate and a child was born to them. She reported the matter to the king.

The king wanted to know if she could prove their mutual relationship to the general public. She agreed and suggested a plan of action. Accordingly the king announced a public dancing performance by the *dasi* and invited the people to it. The crowd gathered and she also appeared, but not before she had given a dose of physic to the child and left it in charge of the saint at home.

As the dance was at its height, the child was crying at home for its mother. The father took the babe in his arms and went to the dancing performance. As she was dancing hilariously he could not approach her with the child. She noticed the man and the babe, and contrived to kick her legs in the dance, so as to unloose one of her anklets just as she approached the place where the saint was. She gently lifted her foot and he tied the anklet. The public shouted and laughed. But he remained unaffected. Yet to prove his worth, he sang a Tamil song meaning:

"For victory, let go my anger!
I release my mind when it rushes away.
If it is true that I sleep day and
night quite aware of my Self,
may this stone burst into twain
and become the wide expanse!"

Immediately the stone (idol) burst with a loud noise. The people were astounded.

Thus he proved himself an unswerving *jnani*. One should not be deceived by the external appearance of a *jnani*. Verse 181 of *Vedanta Chudamani* further explains this. Its meaning is as follows:

Although a *jivanmukta* associated with the body may, owing to his *prarabdha*, appear to lapse into ignorance or wisdom, yet he is only pure like the ether (*akasa*) which is always itself clear, whether covered by dense clouds or without being covered by clouds. He always revels in the Self alone, like a loving wife taking pleasure with her husband alone. Though she attends on him with things obtained from others (by way of fortune, as determined by her *prarabdha*). Though he remains silent like one devoid of learning, his supineness is due to the implicit duality of the *vaikhari vak* (spoken words) of the Vedas; his silence is the highest expression of the realised non-duality which is after all the true content of the Vedas. Though he instructs his disciples, he does not pose as a teacher in the full conviction that the teacher and disciple are mere conventions born of illusion (*maya*), and so he continues to utter words like *akasvani*. If, on the other hand, he mutters words incoherently like a lunatic, it is because his experience is inexpressible. If his words are many and fluent like those of an orator, they represent the recollection of his experience, since he is the unmoving non-dual One without any desire awaiting fulfilment. Although he may appear grief-stricken like any other man in bereavement, yet he evinces just the right love of and pity for the senses which he earlier controlled before he realised that they were mere instruments and manifestations of the Supreme Being. When he seems keenly interested in the wonders of the world, he is only ridiculing the ignorance born of superimposition. If he appears wrathful he means well to the offenders. All his actions should be taken to be only divine manifestations on the plane of humanity. There should not arise even the least doubt as to his being emancipated while yet alive. He lives only for the good of the world.

TOTAL ABIDANCE

A devotee asked, "How does the repetition of the name of God help Realisation?" Sri Bhagavan replied, "The original name is always going on spontaneously without any effort on the part of the individual. That name is aham *– 'I'. But when it becomes manifest it manifests as* ahamkara *– the ego. The oral repetition of the name leads one to mental repetition which finally resolves itself into the eternal vibration. The mind or the mouth cannot act without the Self." Thereupon Sri Bhagavan told the following story.*

TUKARAM, THE GREAT Maharashtra Saint, used to remain in *samadhi* in the day and sing and dance at night with large crowds of people. He always used to utter the name of Sri Rama. Once he was answering the call of nature and also saying "Ram, Ram". An orthodox priest was shocked at the uttering of the holy name by the saint when his body was not clean. Hence he reprimanded him and ordered him to be silent. Tukaram said, "All right!" and remained mute. But at once there arose the name of Rama from every pore of Tukaram and the priest was horrified by the din. He then prayed to Tukaram, "Restrictions are only for the common people and not for saints like you."

QUIET PIETY

THERE WAS A king with a devoted queen. She was a devotee of Sri Rama and yearned that her husband should similarly be a devotee. One night she found that the king mumbled something in his sleep. She kept her ears close to his lips and heard the word 'Rama' repeated continually as in *japa*. She was delighted and the next day ordered the minister to hold a feast. The king having partaken of the feast asked his wife for an explanation. She related the whole occurrence and said that the feast was in gratitude to God for the fulfilment of a long cherished wish. The king was however annoyed that his devotion should have been found out. Some say that having thus betrayed God he considered himself unworthy of God and so committed suicide. It means that one should not openly display one's piety. We may take it that the king told the queen not to make a fuss over his piety and they then lived happily together.

Unknown Tenth Man

D. Not having realised the Truth that the Self alone exists, should I not adopt bhakti *and* yoga margas *as being more suitable for purposes of* sadhana *than* vichara marga? *Is not the Realization of one's Absolute Being that is,* Brahma jnana, *something quite unattainable to a layman like me?*

M. Brahma jnana is not a knowledge to be acquired, so that acquiring it one may obtain happiness. It is one's ignorant outlook that one should give up. The Self you seek to know is verily yourself. Your supposed ignorance causes you needless grief like that of the ten foolish men who grieved the 'loss' of the tenth man who was never lost.

THE TEN FOOLISH men in the parable forded a stream and on reaching the other shore wanted to make sure that all of them had in fact safely crossed the stream. One of the ten began to count, but while counting others left himself out. "I see only nine; sure enough we have lost one. Who can it be?" he said. "Did you count correctly?" asked another, and did the counting himself. But he too counted only nine. One after the other each of the ten counted only nine, missing himself. "We are only nine" they all agreed, "but who is the missing one?", they asked themselves. Every effort they made to discover the 'missing' individual failed. "Whoever he be that is drowned" said the sentimental of ten fools, "we have lost him". So saying he burst into tears, and the rest of the nine followed suit. Seeing them weeping on the river bank, a sympathetic wayfarer enquired for the cause. They related what had happened and said that even after counting themselves several times they could find no more than nine. On hearing the story, but seeing all the ten before him, the wayfarer guessed what had happened. In order to make them know for themselves that they were really ten, that all of them had come safe from the crossing, he told them, "Let each of you count for himself but one after the other serially, one, two, three and so on, while I shall give you each a blow so that all of you may be sure of having been included in the count, and included only once. The tenth 'missing' man will then be found." Hearing this they rejoiced at the prospect of finding their 'lost' comrade and accepted the method suggested by the wayfarer.

While the kind wayfarer gave a blow to each of the ten in turn, he that got the blow counted himself aloud. "Ten" said the last man as he got the last blow in his turn. Bewildered they looked at one another, "We are ten" they said with one voice and thanked the wayfarer for having removed their grief.

That is the parable. From where was the tenth man brought in? Was he ever lost? By knowing that he had been there all the while, did they learn anything new? The cause of their grief was not the real loss of any one of the ten, it was their own ignorance, rather their mere supposition that one of them was lost – though they could not find who he was – because they counted only nine.

GOD WORKS FOR HIS DEVOTEE

ON A PARTICULAR day in the year the God and the Goddess are taken to an adjoining field and the festival of the gods and goddess is celebrated. This is in memory of the fact that one day Sundaramurti Swami entered the temple and found to his dismay that neither God nor Goddess was there, and that on searching for them he found them in a field working at transplanting seedlings for a devotee, a *Harijan*.

EACH REFLECTS HIS OWN NATURE

A NAYANAR WENT to Kalahasti for the *darsan* of God. He saw all the people there as Siva, and Sakti, because he Himself was so. Again Dharmaputra considered that the whole world was composed of people having some merit or other and that each of them was even better than he himself for some reason or other. Whereas Duryodhana could not find even a single good person in the world. Each reflects his own nature.

THE MASTER'S PAYMENT

A DISCIPLE SERVED his master for a long time and realised the Self. He was in Bliss and wanted to express his gratitude to the Master. He was in tears of joy and his voice choked when he spoke. He said, "What a wonder that I did not know my very Self all these years! I suffered long and you so graciously helped me to realise the Self. How shall I repay your grace? It is not in my power to do it." The Master replied, "Well, well. Your repayment consists in not lapsing into ignorance again but in continuing in the state of your real Self."

THE FAULT LIES IN EXPOSURE

EZHUTHACHAN, A GREAT saint and author, had a few fish concealed on him when he entered the temple. The saint was searched and taken to the king. The king asked him, "Why did you take the fish into the temple?" He replied, "It is not my fault. I had it concealed in my clothes. The others exposed the fish in the temple. The fault lies in exposure. Excreta within the body are not considered filthy; but when excreted, they are considered filthy. So also with this."

BRAHMACHARI'S TOUCH

SRI BHAGAVAN WARNED the hearers against the mistake of disparaging a *jnani* for his apparent conduct and again cited the story of Parikshit. He was a still born child. The ladies cried and appealed to Sri Krishna to save the child. The sages round about wondered how Krishna was going to save the child from the effects of the arrows (*apandavastra*) of Asvattama. Krishna said, "If the child be touched by one eternally celibate (*nityabramachari*) the child would be brought to life." Even Suka dared not touch the child. Finding no one among the reputed saints bold enough to touch the child, Krishna went and touched it, saying, "If I am eternally celibate (*nityabramachari*) may the child be brought to life." The child began to breathe and later grew up to be Parikshit.

Just consider how Krishna surrounded by 16,000 gopis is a *brahmachari*! Such is the mystery of *jivanmukti*! A *jivanmukta* is one who does not see anything separate from the Self.

THE KING AND HIS MINISTERS

D: *What is the difference between a man who makes no attempt and remains an* ajnani, *and another who gains a glimpse and returns to* ajnana?

M: *In the latter case a stimulus is always present to goad him on to further efforts until the Realisation is perfect.*

D: *The* Srutis *say, 'this knowledge of* Brahman *shines forth once and for ever'.*

M: *They refer to the permanent Realisation and not to the glimpse.*

D: *How is it possible that a man forgets his own experience and falls back into ignorance?*

Sri Bhagavan illustrated this with the following story.

THERE WAS A king who treated his subjects well. One of his ministers gained his confidence and misused the influence. All the other ministers and officers were adversely affected and they hit upon a plan to get rid of him. They instructed the guards not to let the man enter the palace. The king noted his absence and enquired after him. He was informed that the man was taken ill and could not therefore come to the palace. The king deputed his physician to attend on the minister. False reports were conveyed to the king that the minister was sometimes improving and at other times collapsing. The king desired to see the patient. But the pandits said that such an action was

32

against the *dharma*. Later the minister was reported to have died. The king was very sorry when he heard the news.

The arrogant minister was kept informed of all the happenings by spies of his own. He tried to foil the other ministers. He waited for the king to come out of the palace so that he might report himself to the king. On one occasion he climbed up a tree, hid himself among the branches and awaited the king. The king came out that night in the palanquin and the man in hiding jumped down in front of the palanquin and shouted his identity. The companion of the king was equally resourceful. He at once took out a handful of sacred ashes (*vibhuti*) from his pocket and scattered it in the air so that the king was obliged to close his eyes. The companion also shouted victory (*jai*) to the king and ordered the band to play so that the other man's shout was drowned in the noise. He also ordered the palanquin-bearers to move fast and he himself sang incantations to keep off evil spirits. The king was thus left under the impression that the dead man's ghost was playing pranks with him.

The disappointed man became desperate and retired into the forest for *tapasya* (austerities). After a long time the king happened to go hunting. He came across the former minister seated in deep contemplation. But he hastened away from the spot lest the ghost should molest him.

THE GREATNESS OF *JAPA*

A devotee asked, "Swami, what is the easiest way to attain moksha?"

Bhagavan said with a smile, "As and when the mind goes astray, it should be turned inward and made to steady itself in the thought of the Self. That is the only way."

Another devotee said, "To do so, the repeating of the name of Rama is good, is it not?"

"Certainly, it is good," said Bhagavan. "What could be better? The greatness of the japa *of the name of Rama is extraordinary. In the story of Namadeva he is reported to have told one devotee, 'If you want to know the greatness of the name of Rama you must first know what your own name is, what your real nature* (swarupa) *is, who you are and how you were born. Unless you know your own origin, you will not know your name!' This idea is found in the* Abhangas *of Namadeva written in Marathi language and in the Malayalam* Adhyatma Ramayana." *Thereupon Bhagavan related a story from the latter.*

IT IS STATED in that book that when Anjaneya went in search of Sita, he seated himself opposite to Ravana in the *Darbar* Hall on a high pedestal and fearlessly spoke to him thus: 'Oh Ravana, I give you a teaching (*upadesa*) for attaining liberation (*moksha*). Please listen to me carefully. It is certain that the Self (*Atma*) gets purified by intense devotion to Hari, who is in the lotus of the Heart at all times. The ego gets destroyed and then the sin gets destroyed. Afterwards, in its place, the knowledge of the transcendent Self emerges. With a pure mind and with the Bliss (*Ananda*) generated by a firm knowledge of the Self, the two letters 'Ra' 'Ma' which are like *mantras*, will repeat themselves within you automatically. What more is required for a person who has this knowledge, however little it might be? Hence worship the lotus feet of Vishnu, which will remove all worldly fears, which are dear to all devotees and which shine as brightly as the light of a crore of Suns. Give up the ignorance of your mind'. This has been mentioned in two or three *slokas* in the Sanskrit *Adhyatma Ramayanam* but not as elaborately as in the Malayalam text. Is the greatness of the name of Rama ordinary?

SILENT ELOQUENCE

Lakshman Brahmachari from Sri Ramakrishna Mission asked, "Enquiry of 'Who am I?' or of the 'I-thought' being itself a thought, how can it be destroyed in the process?" Sri Bhagavan replied with a story.

WHEN SITA WAS asked who was her husband among the *rishis* (Rama himself being present there as a *rishi*) in the forest, by the wives of the *rishis*, she denied each one as he was pointed out to her, but simply hung down her head when Rama was pointed out. Her silence was eloquent.

Similarly, the Vedas also are eloquent in *neti-neti* (not this, not this) and then remain silent. Their silence is the Real State. This is the meaning of exposition by silence. When the source of the 'I'-thought is reached it vanishes and what remains is the Self.

HEADSHIP OF A *MUTT*

A devotee told Bhagavan about his ill-health, treatment by doctors and services rendered to him by his servants. Bhagavan did not immediately reply to him, but in the evening, when the devotees all gathered, he began massaging his own legs with oil. Looking at the questioner with a smile, he said, "We are our own doctors and our own servants." The questioner then said, "What are we to do if we do not have strength like Bhagavan to attend to our own work?" Bhagavan's reply was, "If we have strength to eat, why should we not have strength to do this?" The questioner could not say anything and so kept silent with his head bent. Just then the post arrived. After looking through the letters, Bhagavan narrated the following story.

ONCE A CERTAIN *sanyasi* was anxious to be the head of a *Mutt*. He had to have disciples, you see and he tried his level best to secure some. Anyone who came, soon found out the limited knowledge of the person and so went away. No one stayed on. What could he do?

One day he had to go to a city. There he had to keep up his position; but he had no disciple. No one must know this. His bundle of clothes, etc., was on his head. So, he thought he would place the bundle in some house unobserved and then pretend to go there afterwards. He wandered throughout the place. Whenever he tried to step into a house, he found a number of people in front of it. Poor chap! What could he do? It was almost evening. He was tired. At last he found a house with no one in front. The door was open. Greatly relieved, he placed the bundle in one corner of the house and then sat in the verandah.

After a while the lady of the house came out and enquired who he was. "Me! I am the head of a *Mutt* in such and such a place. I came to this city on some work. I heard that you were good householders. I therefore sent my belongings through my disciple to put them in your house thinking that we could put up with you for the night and go away next morning. Has he done so?" "No one has come sir", she said. "No, please. I asked him to put the bundle here, go to the bazaar and get some things. Kindly see if he has put it in any corner", he said. When the lady searched this side and that, she saw the bundle in one corner. Thereupon she and her husband welcomed him and gave him food, etc.

Rather late in the night, they asked, "How is it, sir your disciple has not come yet?" He said, "Perhaps that useless fellow has eaten something in the bazaar and is wandering about. You please go to bed. If he comes, I will open the door for him."

That couple had by then understood the *sanyasi's* true position. They thought they would see further fun and so went into the house to lie down. Then the person started his acting. He opened the door and closed it, making a loud noise so as to be heard by the members of the household. He then said loudly, "Why! What have you been doing so long? Take care – if you do it again, I shall beat you black and blue. Be careful henceforth." Changing his tone thereafter, he said in a plaintive voice, "Swami, Swami, please excuse me. I shall not do it again." Assuming the original tone, he said, "All right. Come here, massage my legs here. No, there. Please hit lightly with your fists. Yes a little more." So saying, he massaged his own legs and then said, "Enough. It is rather late. Go to bed." So saying he went to sleep. There was a hole in the wall of the room where the couple were staying and through it they saw the whole farce.

In the early morning the *sanyasi* again began repeating the evening's performance, saying, "You lazy fellow! The cocks have begun to crow. Go to so and so's house and come back after doing such and such work." So saying, he opened the door, pretended to send him away and went back to bed. The couple saw this also.

In the morning he bundled up his belongings, put the bundle in a corner, and went to a tank nearby for bathing, etc. The couple took the bundle and hid it somewhere. The *sannyasi* returned and searched the whole room but the bundle was not found anywhere. So he asked the lady of the house, "Where is my bundle?" The couple then replied, "Sir, your disciple came here and took away the bundle saying you wanted him to bring it to you. It is the same person who massaged your legs last night. He must be round the corner. Please see, Swami." What could he do then? He kept his mouth shut and started going home.

This is what happens if a disciple serves you. Just like me, we are our own servants.

So saying, Bhagavan pretended to massage his legs with his hands and his fists.

BHAKTA EKANATH

A discussion in the hall centred on the story of Kulasekhara Alwar, which had appeared in the Vision *magazine. During a* Harikatha, *Kulasekhara identifying himself so completely with the situation of the story, felt it his duty as a worshipper of Rama to at once hasten to Lanka and release Sita. He ran to the sea and entered it to cross over to Lanka, when Rama appeared with Sita and Lakshmana and showered His grace on him. This led others in the hall to remark, "Some Maratha saint also did a similar thing. He leaped up to the roof, I think." Thereupon Sri Bhagavan related the story.*

EKANATH WAS WRITING the *Ramayana*, and when he came to the portion in which he was graphically describing that Hanuman jumped across the ocean to Lanka, he so identified himself with his hero Hanuman that unconsciously he leaped into the air and landed on the roof of his neighbour's house. This neighbour had always had a poor opinion of Ekanath, taking him for a humbug and religious hypocrite. He heard a thud on his roof, and coming out to see what it was, discovered Ekanath lying down on the roof with a cadjan leaf in one hand and his iron stile in the other. The cadjan leaf had verses describing how Hanuman leapt across the sea. This incident proved to the neighbour what a genuine *bhakta* Ekanath was and he became his disciple.

After a pause Bhagavan also related: "God appeared in a dream to Ekanath and asked him to go and repair the tomb of Jnaneswar. When Ekanath went there accordingly, he found a contractor ready to do all the work and take payment at the end. The contractor opened a big account in which all expenses were entered, with the names of all the workmen and wages paid. Everything went on systematically. When the work of repairs was completed, the accounts were looked into and the contractor paid his dues. Then the contractor and his big account book totally disappeared. Then alone Ekanath came to know that God was his contractor and did the work. Such things have happened."

THE IMMATURE POT

D: *Is it possible to speak to Iswara as Sri Ramakrishna did?*

M: *When we can speak to each other why should we not speak to Iswara in the same way?*

D: *Then why does it not happen with us?*

M: *It requires purity and strength of mind and practice in meditation.*

D: *Does God become evident if the above conditions exist?*

M: *Such manifestation is as real as your own reality. In other words, when you identify yourself with the body as in* jagrat *you see gross objects; when in subtle body or in mental plane as in* swapna, *you see objects equally subtle; in the absence of identification as in* sushupti *you see nothing. The objects seen bear a relation to the state of the seer. The same applies to visions of God.*

By long practice the figure of God, as meditated upon, appears in dream and may later appear in jagrat *also.*

D: *Is that the state of God-realisation?*

M: *Listen to what happened once years ago.*

Vithoba found Namdev had not yet realised the Supreme Truth and wanted to teach him. When Jnaneswar and Namdev returned from their pilgrimage, Gora Kumbhar gave a feast to all the saints in his place and among them were Jnaneswar and Namdev. At the feast Jnaneswar, in collusion with Gora, told Gora publicly, "You are a potter, daily engaged in making pots and testing them to see which are properly baked and which are not. These pots before you (i.e., the saints) are the pots of *Brahma*. See which of these are sound and which not." Thereupon Gora said, "Yes, Swami, I shall do so," and took up the stick with which he used to tap his pots to test their soundness. Holding it aloft in his hand he went to each of his guests and tapped each on the head as he usually did to his pots. Each guest humbly submitted to such tapping. But when Gora approached Namdev, the latter indignantly called out, "You potter, what do you mean by coming to tap me with that stick?" Gora thereupon told Jnaneswar, "Swami, all the other pots have been properly baked. This one (i.e. Namdev) alone is not yet properly baked." All the assembled guests burst into laughter.

Namdev felt greatly humiliated and ran up to Vitthala (the deity he worshipped) with whom he was on the most intimate terms, playing with him, eating with him, sleeping with him and so on. Namdev complained of this humiliation which had happened to him, the closest friend and companion of Vitthala. Vitthala (who of course knew all this) pretended to sympathise with him, asked for all the details of the happenings at Gora's house and after hearing everything said, "Why should you not have kept quiet and submitted to the tapping, as all the others did? That is why all this trouble has come." Thereupon Namdev cried all the more and said, "You also want to join the others and humiliate me. Why should I have submitted like the others? Am I not your closest friend, your child?" Vitthala said, "You have not yet properly understood the truth, and you won't understand if I tell you. But go to the saint who is in a ruined temple in such and such a forest. He will be able to give you enlightenment."

Namdev accordingly went there and found an old, unassuming man sleeping in a corner of the temple with his feet on a *Sivalingam*. Namdev could hardly believe this was the man from whom he – the companion of Vitthala – was to gain enlightenment. However, as there was none else there, Namdev went near the man and clapped his hands. The old man woke up with a start and seeing Namdev, said, "Oh – you are Namdev whom Vitthala has sent here. Come!" Namdev was dumbfounded and began to think, "This must be a great man." Still he thought it was revolting that any man however great, should be resting his feet on a *lingam*. He asked the old man, "You seem to be a great personage. But is it proper for you to have your feet on a *lingam?*" The old man replied, "Oh, are my feet on a *lingam?* Where is it? Please remove my feet elsewhere." Namdev removed the feet and put them in various places. Wherever they were put, there was a *Sivalingam*. Finally, he took them on his lap and he himself became a *Sivalingam!* Then he realised the truth and the old gentleman said, "Now you can go back."

Bhagavan added, "It is to be noted that only when he surrendered himself, and touched the feet of his guru, enlightenment came. After this final enlightenment Namdev returned to his house and for some days did not go to Vitthala at the temple, though it had been his habit not only to visit Vitthala every day, but to spend most of his time with Vitthala at the temple. So, after a few days, Vitthala went to Namdev's house and like a guileless soul, enquired how it was that Namdev had forgotten him and never visited him. Namdev replied, 'No more of your fooling me. I know now. Where is the place where you are not! To be with you, should I go to the temple? Do I exist apart from you?' Then Vitthala said, 'So you now understand the truth. That is why you had to be sent for this final lesson'."

TAPO BHRASHTA

(Fallen from the state of *tapas*)

NAKKIRAR WAS DOING *tapas* on the bank of a *tirtha*. A leaf fell down from the tree; half the leaf touched the water and the other half touched the ground. Suddenly the water-half became a fish and the land-half became a bird. Each of them was united to the other by the leaf and struggled to go into its own element. Nakkirar was watching it in wonder and suddenly a spirit came down from above and carried him away to a cave where there were already 999 captives, all of whom were *tapo bhrashtas*.

Devotee: "Was Nakkirar a *tapo bhrashta*?"

Bhagavan: "Yes. While engaged in contemplation, why did he fall from contemplation and take to watching the mysterious happening in front of him? Nakkirar composed *Tirumurukatruppadai* and obtained the release of all the thousand prisoners."

YOGI'S PENANCE

Bhagavan narrated the following story to illustrate the distinction between manolaya *(stillness of mind) and* manonasa *(destruction of mind).*

A YOGI WAS doing penance (*tapas*) for a number of years on the banks of the Ganges. When he had attained a high degree of concentration, he believed that to remain in that state for prolonged periods constituted salvation and therefore continued practising it. One day, before going into *samadhi* (a state of deep concentration), he felt thirsty and asked his disciple to bring some water for drinking from the Ganges; but before the disciple could return with the water, he had gone into *samadhi*, and he remained in that state for countless years. When he woke up from this experience, the first thing he did was to say, "water! water!"; but there was neither his disciple nor the Ganges in sight.

The first thing which he asked for was water because, before going into deep concentration, the topmost thought in his mind was about water; by concentration, however deep and prolonged it might have been, he had only been able to lull his thoughts temporarily; therefore when he revived consciousness this topmost thought flew up with all the speed and force of a flood breaking through the dykes. If this was the case with regard to a thought which took shape immediately before he sat for meditation, there is no doubt that other thoughts which had taken deeper root earlier would still remain unannihilated. If annihilation of thoughts is salvation, can he be said to have attained salvation?

The moral is that one should not be taken away by the spell of temporary stillness but pursue the enquiry till the last *vasana* is eradicated.

BRAHMIN'S CURSE

ONE DAY A sage called Pakanar was weaving a basket in front of his house. Hearing a loud voice chanting, "Hare Ram", he asked his sister who it was that was chanting. His sister replied that it was a *brahmin* who is keeping his own daughter. Pakanar replied, "You are the hundredth person to repeat the scandal". Meanwhile, the *brahmin* having come to that place, the sage told the *brahmin* that his curse was lifted and that he could return home. Later, he explained to his sister thus: "This *brahmin* was living with his widowed daughter. They were generous and kind-hearted. They would invite *sadhus* and feed them with love. On hearing of their generosity a *sadhu* came to visit them. He was well received and fed. The *sadhu* was immensely pleased with their devotion and decided to bless them.

He just glanced once and knew what was in store for them when they die. He called the *brahmin* and told him that after his death he would be tortured by a mountain of leeches in hell. On hearing this, the *brahmin* fell at his feet in terror and implored him for some means of escape. The *sadhu* told him, 'Once while you were cooking food a leech fell from the roof into the cooking pot and died unobserved. You offered that food to a realised sage. Since whatever is given to a sage will be received back a thousand-fold a mountain of leeches are in store for you'. The *sadhu* then advised the *brahmin* that in order to escape this fate he should conduct himself towards his grown-up widowed daughter in such a way, as to provoke a scandal that he was having illicit intimacy with her. He assured him that when a hundred persons had uttered the scandal the sin would leave him completely, having been distributed among the scandal-mongers. The *brahmin* did accordingly and you are the

47

hundredth person to tell the scandal. So I say that the *brahmin's* curse is now removed."

Sri Bhagavan drew from the story the following moral: "Have the best intention, but act in such a way not to win praise, but to incur blame. Resist the temptation to justify yourself even when you are just."

KABIR

KABIR WAS A great *bhakta* (devotee) who lived in or near Benares some centuries ago. Although he had *siddhis* (psychic powers), he earned his livelihood by weaving. One day, when he was working on his loom, a disciple entered in great excitement and said, "Sir, there is a juggler outside here who is attracting large crowds by making his stick stand in the air". Thereupon Kabir, who like all true saints, discouraged the display of jugglery, wanted to shame the man, and so rushed out with a big ball of thread in his hand. Seeing the long bamboo standing in the air, he threw his ball of thread up in the air. As the ball went up it unwound itself till the whole length of thread stood stiff in mid-air, and to a far greater height than the juggler's stick, without any support whatever. The people, including the juggler himself, were stunned with amazement, and Sri Bhagavan's eyes acted the amazement, while his hand stood high above his head in the position of Kabir when he threw up the ball.

KAMAL, SON OF SAINT KABIR

A devotee asked, "Can the place between the eyebrows be said to be the seat of the Self?" Bhagavan replied, "The fact is that a sadhaka *may have his experience at any centre or* chakra *on which he concentrates his mind. But, that particular place of his experience does not for that reason become* ipso facto, *the seat of the Self. There is an interesting story about Kamal, the son of Saint Kabir, which serves as an illustration to show that the head (and a part of the space between the eyebrows) cannot be considered the seat of the Self."*

KABIR WAS INTENSELY devoted to Sri Rama, and he never failed to feed those who sang the praise of the Lord with devotion. On one occasion, however, it so happened that he had not the wherewithal to provide food for a large gathering of devotees. For him, however, there could be no alternative except that he must somehow make every necessary arrangement before the next morning. So he and his son set out at night to secure the required provisions.

The story goes that after the father and son had removed the provisions from a merchant's house through a hole they made in the wall, the son went in again just to wake up the household and tell them, as a matter of principle, that their house had been burgled. When, having roused the household, the boy tried to make good his escape through the hole and join his father on the other side, his body got stuck in the aperture. To avoid being identified by the pursuing household (because, if detected, there would be no feeding at all of the devotees the next day), he called out to his father and told him to sever his head and take it away with him. That done, Kabir made good his escape with the stolen provisions and his son's head, which on reaching home was hidden away from possible detection.

The next day Kabir gave a feast to the *bhaktas*, quite unmindful of what had happened the previous night. "If it is Rama's Will," said Kabir to himself, "that my son should die, may it prevail!" In the evening after the feast, Kabir set out with his party as usual in procession into the town with *bhajana*, etc.

Meanwhile, the burgled householder reported to the king, producing the truncated body of Kamal, which gave them no clue. In order to secure its identification, the king had the body tied up prominently on the highway so that whoever claimed it or took it away (for no dead body is forsaken without the last rites being given to it by the kith and kin) might be interrogated or arrested by the police, who were posted secretly for the purpose.

Kabir and his party came along the highway with the *bhajana* in full swing when, to the astonishment of all, Kamal's truncated body (which was considered dead as a door-nail) began to clap its hands, marking time to the tune sung by the *bhajana* party.

This story disproves the suggestion that the head or the place between the eyebrows is the seat of the Self. It may also be noted that when in the battlefield the head of a soldier in action is severed from the body by a sudden and powerful stroke of the sword, the body continues to run or move its limbs as in a mock fight, just for a while, before it finally falls down dead.

A devotee protested: "But Kamal's body was dead hours before."

Bhagavan replied: "What you call death is really no extraordinary experience for Kamal. Here is the story of what happened when he was younger still."

51

As a boy Kamal had a friend of equal age with whom he used to play games of marbles etc. A general rule they observed between themselves was that if one of them owed the other a game or two, the same should be redeemed the next day. One evening they parted with a game to the credit of Kamal. Next day, in order to claim "the return of the game", Kamal went to the boy's house, where he saw the boy laid on the verandah, while his relatives were weeping beside him. "What is the matter?" Kamal asked them. "He played with me last evening and also owes me a game." The relatives wept all the more saying that the boy was dead. "No," said Kamal, "he is not dead but merely pretends to be so, just to evade redeeming the game he owes me." The relatives protested, asking Kamal to see for himself that the boy was really dead, that the body was cold and stiff. "But all this is a mere pretension of the boy, I know. What if the body be stiff and cold? I too can become like that." So saying Kamal laid himself down and in the twinkling of an eye was dead.

The poor relatives who were weeping till then for the death of their own boy, were distressed and dismayed, and now began to weep for Kamal's death also. But up rose Kamal on his back, declaring, "Do you see it now? I was as you would say dead, but I am up again, alive and kicking. This is how he wants to deceive me, but he cannot elude me like this with his pretensions."

In the end, the story goes, Kamal's inherent saintliness gave life to the dead boy, and Kamal got back that was due to him. The moral is that the death of the body is not the extinction of the Self. The Self is not limited by birth and death, and its place in the physical body is not circumscribed by one's experience felt at a particular place, as for instance between the eyebrows, due to practice of *dhyana* made on that centre. The supreme State of Self-awareness is never absent; it transcends the three states of the mind as well as life and death.

Mutual Curse

INDRA APPROACHED AHALYA (wife of Gautama) taking the form of Gautama and she yielded without knowing that he was not her husband. Without ascertaining the truth, Gautama cursed her to become a stone. Angered thereby Ahalya said, "Oh, you fool of a *Muni*! Without enquiring into the truth, you have cursed me and have not even stated when I shall be free from the curse. Tell me, when will the curse end and how? Why not have some consideration for me and tell me at least that?" Gautama thereupon told her that she would be released from the curse at the time of Rama *avatar* when the dust from Rama's feet fell on her. Immediately thereafter she became a stone.

Gautama left that place and tried to get into his daily rituals but he could not, for he had no peace of mind. He tried his level best but could not control his mind and became more and more troubled. On thinking deeply over the matter, he realised that he had cursed his wife Ahalya without proper enquiry and also recollected that she had in turn cursed him by saying, "You fool of a *Muni*!" After all, she was also a great *tapasvini* (a female ascetic). Hence those words which were unusual must have resulted in an irrevocable curse on himself. He therefore decided to seek the help of *Iswara*, by seeing his "Nataraja Dance", in order to get relieved of the curse.

He therefore went to Chidambaram. At that place he heard an ethereal voice saying, "I shall be pleased to give you *darsan* of my *Thandava* dance in Trisulapura." Gautama immediately left that place and went on foot towards Trisulapura. On nearing the place, and at the mere sight of it, even from a distance, his mind began to get clear. He stayed there for a very long time doing *tapas*. At last *Iswara* was pleased and gave him *darsan* of his "Nataraja Dance" in the month of *Dhanus* when the *Ardra* star was predominant. It was at that time Gautama is reported to have lived under the tree and performed *tapas*. After seeing the dance of *Iswara*, Gautama worshipped *Iswara*, went to his original place and began to perform his rituals as usual.

Later on Ahalya became purified by the dust of the feet of Sri Rama and regained her normal form.

Devotee: "The statement that Ahalya turned into a stone applies only to her mind and not to her body. Is that not so?"

Bhagavan: "That is so. If it is not for the mind, could it be for the body? It is only ordinary people that say her body turned into a stone and that Rama restored her to her original form by putting his foot on the stone. How is that possible? It only means that the mind lost its awareness of the Self, and unable to think of anything else, she became dull like a stone. That dullness got relieved by the *darsan* of a great personage. As she herself was a great *tapasvini* she could immediately become aware of the Self. She worshipped Sri Rama as the embodiment of the Self. This inner meaning could be found in the *Ramayana*. The moment Rama set his foot in Gautamasrama, the mind of Ahalya was restored to its original state, like the blossoming of a flower."

THE LORD HIMSELF COMES

A new Tamil translation of Sankara's Atmabodha *with a commentary was sent to the Ashram. After glancing through it, Bhagavan sent it to the library. It was noticed that Bhagavan did not seem pleased with the translation. Sending for a copy of Sankara's* Atmabodha *from the library, Bhagavan began looking intently into it and after two days rendered two slokas into Tamil verse and showed them to the devotees. Overjoyed at seeing Bhagavan's translation they asked him to finish the whole work. Although Bhagavan said, "Why, why?" he wrote some more saying, "though I feel disinclined to compose more verses, one after another comes and stands in front of me. What am I to do?"*

Little by little the verses continued till all of them were translated. Addressing Sri Muruganar, Bhagavan with a smile said, "How is it I feel I have read this before? Is it possible that someone has already written this?" Muruganar answered, "No one has written it in venba *metre. What surprise is there, if one verse after another occurs to Bhagavan. It is said that in every* kalpa *the Vedas appeared as though they were standing before Brahma. This also is like that."*

JAYADEVA'S STORY IS found in Panduranga Bhakta Vijayam. After writing the Gita Govindam, Jayadeva wrote Bhagavatam also in Sanskrit. On hearing about that, Krauncha Raja appealed to Jayadeva to read the Gita Govindam in the durbar hall and so he began reading it. People who heard him were so impressed with the writing and with his discourses that his fame spread in all directions and people came in large numbers to hear him. His fame spread so far that Jagannatha Swami, the presiding deity of Puri, was eager to listen to him. So he started in the guise of a *brahmin* one day while the discourse was going on and entered the durbar hall of the king. After blessing the king, he said, "Sir, I am a resident of Gokula Brindavan. I am a pandit well versed in all *sastras*. I have been searching all the world over for someone who could discuss the *sastras* with me on equal terms but so far I have not found any one. I am therefore itching for a discussion. I learned that Jayadeva was with you and so I came here. Where is he?" and when the people pointed out Jayadeva to him, he said, disdainfully, "Oh! You are Jayadeva. Let me see. Let us discuss any one of the *sastras* you have studied," and looking at him steadily, said, "What is that in your hands?" Without waiting for a reply, he snatched the book from his hands and said, "Oho! This is *Bhagavatam*. So you are a *Pauranika*? (one who gives discourses on the epics). Who wrote this?" With fear and devotion Jayadeva said, "Sir, I am not a pandit to hold discussions with you. I humbly seek the blessings of elders like you. Though I do not have the courage to say before you that, I wrote this book, still as it will be a fault not to tell you the truth, I admit that I am its author." That *brahmin* pretended surprise and said, "What! If it is you who wrote it, tell me, how could I have learnt all its contents by heart?" So saying and without opening the book he began repeating the contents quickly, chapter by chapter. The king and the audience were amazed. Realising that Lord Jagannatha Himself had come in that form to shower His grace on him, Jayadeva prayed to him to reveal His real form (of Vishnu) with the conch, mace, *chakra* (discus) etc. Pleased with the *stotras* (prayers), Lord Jagannatha revealed Himself in the various forms in which Jayadeva had invoked Him in his *stotras*, blessed him and disappeared.

DELIVERANCE OF A THORN BUSH

One of the devotees who had heard of the verses written by Bhagavan about the deliverance of Lakshmi, the cow, approached Him and said, "Swami, we ourselves see that animals and birds are getting deliverance in your presence; but is it not true that only human beings can get moksha?"

"Why? It is stated that a great saint gave moksha *to a thorn bush," said Bhagavan with a smile. The devotee eagerly asked who that great saint was and what was the story about the thorn bush.*

IN CHIDAMBARAM, THERE was a *jnani* by the name of Umapathi Sivacharya. He was a poet and also a pandit. As he was in a transcendental state of spirituality (*athita sthithi*), he did not pay much attention to the usual *brahminical* practices. Hence, the *dikshitars* of the place became angry with him, especially since he was a learned man and knew all the precepts of the Hindu religion. They forbade him from living in the village or even visiting the temple. He therefore lived in a small hut built on a raised ground outside the village. A low caste man called Pethan Samban used to supply him with all that he required and also helped him in a general way. As things went on like this, one day, when Pethan was carrying on his head a bundle of firewood to the hut, *Iswara* Himself met him on the way in the guise of the *dikshitar* in charge of the temple. He wrote a verse on a palmyra leaf and gave it to him, telling him that it was to be handed over to Umapathi Sivacharya, and then disappeared.

Pethan gave that verse to Sivacharya, who, on opening it, found in the first line itself the words, "*Adiyarkkadiyen Chitrambalavanan*" (the servant of the devotees, the Lord of Chidambaram). Immediately, he was overwhelmed with devotion and a thrill passed through his body as he read the letter. The gist of the verse was, "A note from Chidambaranathan, the servant of the devotees, to the person who has set up a new establishment, namely Sivacharya. It is your duty to give initiation to this Pethan Samban regardless of caste and to the surprise of all people."

He read the letter and was overwhelmed with joy. In obedience to the orders of the Lord, he initiated Pethan into the order of *sannyasa*, though he belonged to the lowest caste. In due course he gave *nayana diksha* (transmission of Power through the eyes) to Pethan, immediately after which Pethan merged into holy light. Sivacharya himself was immensely surprised at this occurrence and only then understood the wisdom of Pethan.

Enemies of Sivacharya noticed the sacrificial offerings and other things he had for this initiation. They complained to the king that Sivacharya had burnt Pethan to death for some mistake, he might have committed. When the king came there with his retinue to enquire into the complaint, Sivacharya showed the verse of Lord Nataraja and said that he gave initiation to Pethan and that Pethan vanished thereafter in the form of a divine light (*jyoti*). The king was surprised and asked Sivacharya if he could likewise give initiation and *moksha* to the thorn bush nearby. "Yes. What doubt, is there?" said Sivacharya. Accordingly he gave *nayana diksha* to that thorn bush and that too immediately disappeared in pure light (*jyoti*).

The king was still more astonished at that and said, "This looks like some black magic. You said this note had been written by Lord Nataraja. Let us go and ask Him." Sivacharya pointed out that there was a ban on his entering the temple. The king said that would not matter as he himself was accompanying

Sivacharya. Accordingly they started for the temple together. Hearing all this, all the people – the pundits, the common people curious about the whole thing and enemies of Sivacharya who were sure he would be duly punished – flocked to the temple to see the strange sight. The two entered the temple. Out of regard for the king, when *Arathi* (waving of lights) was offered to Lord Nataraja, it was found that on either side of the Lord there stood Pethan and the thorn bush. The pundits were surprised and out of fear and remorse, fell at the feet of Sivacharya requesting him to pardon them for all their faults. They subsequently brought him back into the village with due honours.

Brahma, Vishnu, Siva

Stories of the Hindu trinity Brahma
Vishnu and Siva abound throughout
the scriptural literature of India.
Although these stories are both
entertaining and enlightening Sri Bhagavan
also gives a deeper meaning to them, he says,
"Siva is the Being assuming all forms and the
Consciousness seeing them. That is to say, Siva is
the background underlying both the subject and
the object. Everything has its being in Siva and
because of Siva."

SILENCE IS THE TRUE
UPADESA

Once a devotee came and said that the great sages of the past had travelled extensively preaching the Truth and thus had served the world at large. Similarly, if Bhagavan were to travel thus it would be beneficial to many. Smilingly Bhagavan replied that his being settled in one place was also beneficial and narrated the following story.

BRAHMA, THE LORD of Creation, once lost interest in the work of creation and thought of taking to a life of *tapas*. So, out of his mind he created Sanaka, Sanatkumara, Sanandana and Sanatsujata, with the intention to hand over to them his job in the course of time. They grew up and mastered all the branches of study. Brahma then decided to hand over to them his job and to retire. Sage Narada came to know of his father's intention. Since Narada knew that his brothers were full of dispassion and fit to be initiated into the path of Self-knowledge, he decided to warn them beforehand of Brahma's intention. On hearing this the four brothers, who had no intention to follow the path of action, left home in search of a guru without informing their father. They all proceeded to Vaikunta, the abode of Vishnu. There they saw Lakshmi sitting on Vishnu's couch massaging His Feet. On seeing this they thought, "How can this family man bound by the intimate glance of his consort render us any help in learning *adhyatma vidya*. Look at the splendour of this palace and this city! This is enough. Let us seek the help of Lord Siva."

Lord Siva, who was in Kailas with His family, knew beforehand about their coming and understood their plight. He was sure that they would be disappointed on seeing Him with a family, so taking pity on them He decided to impart spiritual knowledge to them. The kind-hearted Lord left Mount Kailas and taking the youthful form of Dakshinamurti seated Himself with *Chinmudra* under a banyan tree on the Northern side of Lake Manasarovar, on the way by which these disappointed devotees were returning to their homes. When they came and sat before Him, He went into *samadhi*. He was in Perfect Repose. Silence prevailed. They saw Him. The effect was immediate. They fell into *samadhi* and their doubts were cleared.

Silence is the true *upadesa*. It is the perfect *upadesa*. It is suited only for the most advanced. Others are unable to draw full inspiration from it. Therefore they require words to explain the Truth. But Truth is beyond words. It does not admit of explanation. All that is possible to do is only to indicate it.

DAKSHINAMURTI

The Self alone, the Sole Reality,
Exists for ever.
If of yore the First of Teachers
Revealed it through unbroken silence
Say, who can reveal it in spoken words?
— *Ekatma Panchakam,* Sri Bhagavan.

Sri Bhagavan once told the story that follows to Sri Muruganar. This brings out the profound significance of the Supreme Silence in which the First Master, Sri Dakshinamurti is established.

Sri Bhagavan said,
"When the four elderly Sanakadi *rishis* first beheld the sixteen-year-old Sri Dakshinamurti sitting under the banyan tree, they were at once attracted by Him, and understood that He was the real *Sadguru.* They approached Him, did three *pradakshinas* around Him, prostrated before Him, sat at His Feet and began to ask shrewd and pertinent questions about the nature of reality and the means of attaining it. Because of the great compassion and fatherly love (*vatsalya*) which He felt for His aged disciples, the young Sri Dakshinamurti was overjoyed to see their earnestness, wisdom and maturity, and gave apt replies to each of their questions. But as He answered each consecutive question, further doubts arose in their minds and they asked further questions. Thus they continued to question Sri Dakshinamurti for a whole year, and He continued

to clear their doubts through His compassionate answers. Finally, however, Sri Dakshinamurti understood that if He continued answering their questions, more doubts would arise in their minds and their ignorance *(ajnana)* would never end. Therefore, suppressing even the feeling of compassion and fatherly love which was welling up within Him, He merged Himself into the Supreme Silence. Because of their great maturity (which had ripened to perfection through their year-long association with the *Sadguru*), as soon as Sri Dakshinamurti assumed Silence, they too automatically merged into Supreme Silence, the true state of the Self."

Wonderstruck on hearing Sri Bhagavan narrating the story in this manner, Sri Muruganar remarked that in no book was it mentioned that Sri Dakshinamurti ever spoke anything. "But this is what actually happened", replied Sri Bhagavan curtly. From the authoritative way in which Sri Bhagavan replied and from the clear and descriptive way in which He told the story, Sri Muruganar understood that Sri Bhagavan was none other than Sri Dakshinamurti Himself!

BRAHMA'S PRIDE

A family came from a distant place to seek solace from the grief of losing six sons; the last child had recently died. As though Bhagavan had inspired the question, a devotee asked about using pranayama *and other practices to prolong life to enable them to become realised souls,* jnanis.

Bhagavan gently replied, "Yes, people do live long if they do these practices, but does a person become a jnani, *a realised soul, by living long? A realised soul has really no love for his body. For one who is the embodiment of bliss, the body itself is a disease. He will await the time to be rid of the body."*

A devotee said, "Some people say we have lived for fifty years, what more is needed? As though living so long were a great thing!"

"Yes," said Bhagavan with a laugh, "that is so. It is a sort of pride and there is a story about it."

IT SEEMS THAT in the olden days, Brahma once felt proud of the fact that he was long-lived. He went to Vishnu and said, "Do you not see how great a person I am! I am the oldest living person (*chiranjeevi*)." Vishnu told him that was not so and that there were people who had lived much longer than he. When Brahma said that could not be, since he was the creator of all living beings, Vishnu took him with him to show him people older than him.

They went along until, at a certain place, they found Romasa Mahamuni. Vishnu asked him his age and how long he expected to live. "Oho!" said Romasa, "you want to know my age? All right, listen then and I will tell you. This era (*yuga*) consists of so many thousands of years. All these years put together make one day and one night for Brahma. It is according to these calculations that Brahma's life is limited to one hundred years. When one such Brahma dies, one of the hairs of my body falls out. Corresponding to such deaths as have already occurred, several of my hairs have fallen out, but many more remain. When all my hairs fall out, my life will be over and I shall die."

Very much surprised at that, they went on to Ashtavakra *Mahamuni*, an ascetic with eight distortions in his body. When they told him about all the above calculations, he said that when one such Romasa *Mahamuni* dies, one of his own distortions would straighten, and when all the distortions had gone, he would die. On hearing this, Brahma was crestfallen. Similarly, there are many stories. If true realization is attained, who wants this body? For a Realised Soul who enjoys limitless bliss through realization of the Self, why this burden of the body?

SWEET OF SPEECH

SATI DEVI, THE wife of Siva and the daughter of Daksha, gave up her life as she was insulted by her father during the *yajna* performed by him. She was subsequently born to Himavan and Menaka as Parvati. She wanted only Lord Siva as her husband, and to achieve that purpose she set out for doing *tapas*. Menaka, while trying to prevent her from doing so said, "U (no), Ma (give up)." That is how she got the name of Uma. Finding Menaka's dissuasion of no use, Himavan took her to the *tapovana* (hermitage) where Siva was staying in the form of Dakshinamurthy and said, "This little child of mine wants to do *tapas*. Please allow her to be under your care." Seeing Parvati, Siva said, "Why *tapas* at this tender age? Why not go home with father?" Parvati replied, "No, I won't go." Parameswara tried to dissuade her skilfully by saying, "I have conquered *prakriti* (nature) and so could concentrate on this *tapas*. If you are to be here you will be exposed to the ravages of *prakriti*. So please go back." Parvati was equally skilful, so she said, "Oh Lord! You say you have conquered *prakriti*. Without some relationship with *prakriti* how could you do *tapas*? You have just spoken. How could you do that without *prakriti*? How could you walk? Without your knowing it, *prakriti* is occupying your heart. If it is not for the sake of argument, if you are really above the influence of *prakriti*, why are you afraid of my staying here?" Siva was pleased with this and said, "*Ingithagna*! (you who are skilled in thought reading), *Madhurvachani*! (you who are sweet of speech) stay on!" and sent Himavan home.

PARVATI'S TEST

Sri Bhagavan was looking into the Siva Purana *and related, "Siva has the transcendental and immanent aspects as represented by His invisible, transcendental being and the* linga *aspect respectively. The* linga, *manifested as Arunachala originally, stands even to this day.*

"In the sphere of speech, Pranava *(the mystic sound AUM) represents the transcendental* (nirguna), *and the* Panchakshari *(the five-syllabled* mantra), *represents the immanent aspect* (saguna)." *To illustrate this Sri Bhagavan recounted the anecdote of Parvati testing Rama.*

RAMA AND LAKSHMANA were wandering in the forest in search of Sita. Rama was grief-stricken. Just then Siva and Parvati happened to pass close-by. Siva saluted Rama and passed on. Parvati was surprised and asked Siva to explain why He, the Lord of the Universe, being worshipped by all, should stoop to salute Rama, an ordinary human who having missed his consort was grief-stricken and moving in anguish in the wilderness looking helpless. Siva then said, "Rama is simply acting as a human being would under the circumstances. He is nevertheless the incarnation of Vishnu and deserves to be saluted. You may test him if you choose."

Parvati considered the matter, took the shape of Sita and appeared in front of Rama, as he was crying out the name of Sita in great anguish. He looked at Parvati appearing as Sita, smiled and asked, "Why Parvati, are you here? Where is Sambhu? Why have you taken the shape of Sita?" Parvati felt abashed and explained how she went there to test him and sought an explanation for Siva saluting him.

Rama replied, "We are all only aspects of Siva, worshipping Him at sight and remembering Him out of sight."

GOING ROUND THE SELF

In the evening when some devotees were beginning giripradakshina, (circumambulation around the hill Arunachala), Sundaresa Iyer, a long-standing devotee also felt like going with them. Then feeling that he might not be able to complete the round, as the others were taking leave, he quickly went around Bhagavan. Bhagavan asked him why he was doing this. He replied, "I am afraid I cannot go around the hill, so I have gone around Bhagavan." "Go around yourself That will be Atma pradakshina," Bhagavan said with smile.

Another devotee remarked, "It means he has done what Vinayaka once did". Bhagavan was then asked to tell that story.

ONCE UPON A time, Lord Parameswara wanted to teach a lesson to His Son, Lord Subrahmanya. Along with Parvathi, Parameswara sat on the top of Mount Kailas holding a fruit in His hand. Seeing the fruit both Ganapathi and Subrahmanya asked their Father, Parameswara for it. Then *Iswara* said that He would give the fruit to whoever of them returned first after going round the whole world. With self-confidence and pride that he would win the race, Subrahmanya started immediately riding on his favourite mount, the peacock. He began going at a fast pace, frequently looking behind to assure himself that his elder brother Ganapathi was not following. What could poor Ganapathi do, with his huge belly? His *vahanam* (mount) was after all a mouse. So he thought it was no use competing with Subrahmanya in the race round the world, and went round Parvati and Parameswara, bowed before them and claimed the reward. When they asked him whether he had gone round the world, he said, "All the worlds are contained within you; so if I go round you, it is as good as going round the world". Pleased with his reply, Parameswara gave him the fruit and Ganapathi sat there eating it.

By the time Subrahmanya finished going round the world in full confidence that he would be the winner, arriving at the starting point, he found Ganapathi seated before Parvati and Parameswara, eating the fruit. When he asked Parameswara to give him the fruit for winning the race, *Iswara* said, 'There it is, your elder brother is eating it.' When he asked his father how that could be fair, *Iswara* explained to him all that had happened. Subrahmanya then realised his vanity in thinking that he was a great sage, bowed before his parents, and asked to be pardoned. That is the story. The significance is that the ego which goes round like a whirlwind must get destroyed, and must get absorbed in *Atma*. That is *Atma Pradakshina*, said Bhagavan.

ARDHANAREESWARA

(A form of Siva – half man and half woman)

ONCE UPON A time on Mount Kailas, the mountain of delight, the great Lord Siva and Goddess Parvati were sitting on a resplendent throne. The place was filled with the scent of fine flowers and incense. After granting the boons desired by *devas, rishis* and other hosts of devotees, and dismissing them, Lord Siva rejoiced in the company of Goddess Uma (Parvati). The great God pleased Goddess Uma who was as beautiful as goddess Rati and full of auspicious qualities and noble traits. In a joyous mood the Goddess, who thought that her Lord's attention was entirely centred on her, slipped playfully behind Him and in sport covered fondly the three eyes of Sambhu, the Lord of the World, with her two hands resembling lotus petals and asked merrily, "who is it?"

As soon as His three eyes (the Moon, the Sun and Fire) were covered a dismal darkness spread over the universe for millions of years, because half a trice for Siva is aeons for us. The darkness produced by the playfulness of the Goddess proved to be the cause of the untimely destruction of the worlds, for in the dense darkness no activities were possible and consequently living beings perished without giving birth to new generations.

Seeing this state of affairs, the ever glorious *Siddhas* approached Sambhu with devotion and prayed to Him for the well-being of the universe. In response to this prayer of devotees and *Siddhas*, Lord Siva, the embodiment of compassion, said, "Gowri! Leave my eyes alone". Immediately the Goddess removed the obstruction to the Moon, Sun and Fire in the form of the eyes of Hara. Light returned to the worlds. The Lord then asked the *Siddhas*, who stood in an attitude of worship, "How much time has elapsed?" and they replied, "Half a second for you and millions of years for us". On hearing this the Lord, who is an ocean of compassion, turned with a smile to his beloved and graciously spoke some words on *dharma* and *artha*. "It is not proper that you, who are the Mother of the world, should do anything to dissolve it. At the appointed time only I am the one to do so. You have by your folly produced an untimely dissolution. How can you, the embodiment of love, perform acts which cause pain to your creation? You, who are compassion itself, should not even for sport do anything to hurt others".

On hearing Sambhu's words, Uma was struck with remorse and prayed to know what she could do in expiation of this fault of hers. At this Lord Siva was pleased with the repentance and devotion of the Goddess and said, "What penance can be prescribed for you leaving me out? Besides you follow the path of *dharma*. Therefore I shall prescribe a penance for you in accordance with prevailing practice. You may perform meritorious acts for the welfare of *karmabhoomi* (the earth, which is said to be the place most suited for performing religious rites). People will acquire firm faith in *dharma* by seeing your method of doing penance. There is no doubt about it. Your grace will make the earth realize its goal, which is the maintenance of *dharma*, Goddess! The timeless Vedas declare you to be the All. The city known as Kancheepuri is heaven on earth. A little penance done there yields boundless results. I shall remain there in the lotus of your heart in my formless state as the Absolute Pure Being. Therefore you need not suffer the pangs of separation from me". On hearing this, the Goddess at once proceeded southwards with her companions.

At that time, in the kingdom of Kasi there was famine for want of rain, and the people were suffering greatly as they could not get food. Seeing this on Her way and taking pity on the people, Devi created a big mansion by Her mere wish, took the name of Annapurna and, with a vessel which never became empty, fed thousands of people. Before long Her fame spread throughout the country.

Meanwhile the king himself found that his granary had become empty and was wondering what to do. When he heard of the poor-feeding that was being done by this lady Annapurna, he was greatly surprised at the ability of a mere woman and, to test her, asked for the loan of few measures of rice. He received a reply saying that there was no question of lending but that he could come there to eat. With a wish to test her ability, the king and his ministers went there in disguise and ate the food that was given. When the king found the inexhaustibility of the food that was being served all round, he immediately realised that this could not be done by any human agency but only by divine power.

Therefore, after the meal, he went and fell at the feet of Annapurna and prayed, "Great Mother, please bless us and grant us deliverance". Pleased with his devotion, the Divine Mother assumed Her original form and said, "My son, I am pleased with your devotion. As I have stayed here so long, your country will be relieved of the evils of drought. You will now have rain and there will be no famine. I cannot stay here any longer. I must go south for my penance. Rule the people well and be happy". The king prayed, "Even so, You should be available to us for our worship". So the Mother agreed and left. That is the reason why She manifested herself as ANNAPURNA, and the place where She was, is now famous as the Temple of Annapurna.

From there She went to Kancheepuram in the South. There She saw the pure and holy waters of the Kampa and began to practise austerities on the river bank. She put aside Her various ornaments and instead wore beads of *rudraksha*. She threw away Her fine clothes and wore for garments the bark of trees, and smeared her entire body with holy ashes. She lived on ears of corn picked by Herself and always repeated the name of Siva. Thrice a day (morning, noon and evening) She bathed in the Kampa, and lovingly shaped its sand into a Linga. Full of devotion She worshipped it with leaves as traditionally prescribed. She respectfully welcomed the holy sages (*maharshis*) who came to see Her. The sages were filled with wonder at Her austerities.

On one occasion She had collected and cleaned the flowers from the forest. Repeating *mantras* She began to worship the *Linga* made of sand, on the bank of the Kampa, in the *agamic* way. Siva wished to test Her devotion and so made the waters of the Kampa rise and overflow its banks. Seeing a huge flood approaching, Her companions warned Devi, who opened Her eyes and saw the river in spate. Distressed at this obstacle to Her worship, She at once embraced the *Linga* lest it should crumble away and said to them, "What to do? Worship in progress cannot be stopped, come what may. Only those who have acquired merit can bring to completion their good actions in this world and practise the *dharma* which is capable of fulfilling the desires of the heart. The *Sivalinga* is made of sand. It will dissolve in the flood. If a *Linga* is to be destroyed, a true devotee should also perish with it. This flood has risen up through the *maya* of Siva to test the sincerity of my devotion. I will continue without the least fear. Friends! Go away quickly!" Saying this, Ambika did not abandon the *Linga* which She was embracing, even though She was fast being surrounded by water. She devoutly adored the great *Linga*, clasped it to Her heart, and with open eyes meditated on Sadasiva with one pointed devotion.

Then a divine voice from the sky spoke: "Girl! This great flood has subsided. You can now leave the *Linga,* noblest of beings! This *Linga* worshipped by you will achieve everlasting fame as the one worshipped by the gods and capable of granting boons. May your penance be successful! May human beings who see and worship this *Linga* – established for the maintenance of *dharma* – attain the goal of their lives! I myself shine on this earth in the form of the effulgent Arunachala for the liberation of mortals. Since it removes the cruel heap of sins from all the worlds, and since bondage becomes non-existent when one sees it, it is named Arunachala (the Hill that destroys bondage). *Rishis, Siddhas, Gandharvas, Yogis* etc., come here and fervently worship it, forsaking the peaks of Kailas and Mount Meru. You may go there and learn from the Sage Gautama about devotion to me and about the glory of Arunachala, and do more penance. I shall reveal to you my effulgent form there in order that all the sins (of the world) may be destroyed and all the worlds prosper". On hearing these words which came from Siva in His formless state, Devi said, "So be it", and started at once for Arunachala. Turning to the *rishis* who wished to follow Her, She said, "Perform your austerities on the banks of the sacred Kampa. This *Linga* of sand, which removes all sins and brings in all kinds of prosperity, bears the marks of my embrace. Worship it. Let my devotees know that I shall be worshipped as Kamakshi, since I fulfil their desires and bless them. Let them worship me and obtain the boons they desire."

She then came to Arunachala. The Goddess saw *Siddhas, yogis, rishis* and *devas* there. All the Maharshis begged Her to be their guest, but She said that She must see Gautama according to Siva's command. So they directed Her to his ashram. Devi then went to the Gautama Ashram at the foot of the Coral Hill (*pavalakunru*). Satananda, the son of Gautama, saw Her and full of devotional fervour invited and worshipped Her as prescribed and requested Her to stay on while he went to the forest to bring his father, Gautama, who had gone to fetch *Kusa* grass. By that time Gautama had already started for home and when Satananda saw him, he ran to his father with great excitement and told him that the Divine Mother had come to their ashram. The whole forest in the twinkling of an eye became green and full of flowers and fruits. Gautama was surprised and asked his son if it was really so. Satananda with a faltering voice said, "Mother Parvati Herself has come." Equally thrilled and elated, Gautama hastened to the place, saw Parvati and worshipped Her. After Devi performed penance for a long time according to the instructions of Gautama, Mahadeva finally appeared before Her and said that He would grant Her whatever boon She asked for. With great respect Devi prayed that She should become half of Siva Himself saying, "I cannot live any longer with a separate body, for if separate, I may make another mistake like this and then shall have to undergo all the hardships of penance and suffer the pangs of separation". Parameswara therefore acceded to Her request and so united with Her as *ARDHANAREESWARA* (the Lord with a half-female form). This is how Amba, the Mother of the universe, became one half of Siva.

Periapuranam

The *Periapuranam* is a Tamil
devotional classic depicting the lives of
63 *Saivite* Saints. This book made a
remarkable impression on Sri Bhagavan as
a young boy. Speaking of four of the most
famous Saivite Saints Sri Bhagavan once
remarked, "The devotion of Sundaramurthy to
the Lord is that of a friend, of Manikkavachakkar
that of the beloved, of Appar that of a servant and
Sambandar that of a son."

THE FIRE OF DEVOTION

With reference to a devotee's account of the miraculous appearance of sugar candy and almonds, which dropped into the hands of some ladies in a trance, Bhagavan replied, "We hear of so many things. There are certain sects which work for such things. But who sees or gets them? You must see that. In the Periyapuranam *a similar occurrence is mentioned."*

KARAIKAL AMMAIYAR WAS a great devotee of Lord Siva and a poetess, many of whose verses are still preserved. She was the wife of a rich merchant of Karaikal, whose name was Paramadattan (meaning 'one endowed with heavenly gifts'). Her own name was Punithavathiyar (meaning 'the pure one'). She was very devout, and especially eager to entertain all devotees of Lord Siva that came to her door. One day her husband received from some persons who had come to him on business a present of two mangoes of a very superior variety which he sent home to his wife. Soon afterwards, a holy devotee came to her house as a mendicant. Since she had no cooked food ready to offer him except some boiled rice, she gave him one of the aforesaid mangoes along with the rice. At noon her husband returned and after having his meal ate the remaining mango. It pleased him so much that he said to his wife, "There were two, bring me the other." She went away in dismay, but remembering that the Lord to whose servant she had given the fruit, never deserts those who serve Him, she offered a mental prayer, and straightaway found a mango in her hand, which she took to her

81

husband. Being a divine gift, it was of incomparable sweetness, so he asked her, "Where did you obtain this?" She hesitated at first to reveal the wonder that had taken place on her behalf, but thinking that she ought to hide nothing from her husband, she told him everything. He gave no credence to her words, but roughly replied, "If that is so, get me another like it." She went away and said in her heart to God, "If You do not give me one more fruit, my word will have no weight!" Immediately she found another fruit in her hand. She brought this fruit to her husband but as soon as he took it, it disappeared. Wondering at this strange happening, he concluded that his wife must be a divine being and therefore decided that he should no longer live with her. However, he revealed this decision to no one. One day he quietly hired a ship on which he placed a great deal of his wealth, and then on an auspicious day, worshipped the god of the sea. With sailors and a skilful captain, he set sail for another country where, by trading his merchandise he accumulated a fortune. After some time he returned and came to another city in the Pandiyan kingdom, where he married a merchant's daughter and lived in great luxury. A daughter was born to him, whom he named Punithavathi after his first wife, with whom he had feared to remain but for whom he retained great reverence.

After a while, his return and prosperity became known to his friends in Karaikal, who resolved to compel him to receive again his first wife, their kinswoman, whom he had deserted. They accordingly proceeded to his new residence, carrying with them in a litter his saintly spouse, Karaikal Ammaiyar. When he heard that she had arrived and was halting in a grove outside the town, he was seized with great awe. He proceeded with his second wife and daughter to where, she was camping – surrounded by her relatives. He prostrated before her with profoundest reverence, saying, "Your slave is happy here and prosperous through your blessings. To my daughter I have given your sacred name, and I constantly adore you as my tutelary goddess!" Poor Punithavathiyar was utterly confounded by this salutation and worship, and so took refuge among her relatives, who all asked with wonder, "Why is this madman worshipping his own wife?" To this Paramadattan replied, "I myself saw her work a miracle, so I know that she is no daughter of the human race, but a divine being. Therefore I have separated myself from her, and I worship her as my tutelary deity and have dedicated my daughter to her". Hearing this, Punithavathiyar pondered over it and prayed within herself to Siva, the Supreme Lord, saying, "O Lord, this is my husband's belief. So take away from me the beauty that I have till now cherished only for his sake. Remove from me this burden of flesh, and give to me the form and features of those who always attend on Thee, and praise Thee." Immediately, by the grace of God, her flesh dried up and she became a skeleton, becoming one of Siva's hosts whom the earth and the heaven hold in reverence. Then the gods sent down a rain of flowers, heavenly minstrels resounded, and her relatives paid obeisance to her and departed in awe. Having thus assumed the form of a skeleton, she lived in the wild jungle of Alankadu, and through the inspiration of God she sang several sacred poems, which are sung even to this day. After some time there came upon her an irresistible desire to see the sacred Mount Kailas, so with great speed she travelled northwards till she arrived at the foot of the Mountain. Considering that it was not right to tread on the Holy Mountain by foot, she began to climb it with her feet in the air and with only her head touching the ground.

The goddess Uma, Siva's consort, saw her ascending in this manner and said to Her Lord, "Who is this that approaches in this strange fashion, a gaunt skeleton sustained only by the power of love?" Lord Siva replied, "She is Karaikal Ammaiyar, and she has obtained this form by her prayers." When She drew near, He addressed her with words of love, calling her 'Amma' (Mother), a name which she bears ever since. As soon as she heard the word she fell at His feet and exclaimed, "Father!" Siva then said to her, "What boon do you wish to ask from me?" She replied, "O Lord, grant undying love and infinite blessedness to me, Your slave. I would be glad never to be born on earth again, but If I must be so born, grant me at least that I may never, in any form or at any time forget You, my Lord; and when You perform Your sacred mystic dance, may I stand in rapture at Your feet and sing Your praise". The Lord replied, "In Alankadu you shall see my dance, and with rapture you shall sing." Then the holy Karaikal Ammaiyar returned to Alankadu, still covering the distance on her head, and there she beheld the Lord's sacred dance, and sang her renowned lyrics in His praise.

Karaikal Ammaiyar's devotional hymns form sixth part of *Thirumurai*.

MOTHER'S BLESSINGS

SAMBANDHA WAS BORN in an orthodox *brahmin* family in the town of Sirkali, to Sivapada Hridayar and his wife Bhagavatiyar.

One day, when the boy was three years old, the father took him to Thirutonni Appar Koil. The father while immersed in the tank for a bath, began repeating the *aghamarshana mantram*. The child could not see his father in the tank, and looked around in fear and grief. There was no trace of the father. Not able to contain its grief the child wept aloud looking at the temple tower saying, "Mother! Father!" Parvati and Lord Siva appeared in the sky, seated on the sacred bull, and gave *darsan* to the little child. As desired by Siva, Parvati gave the child a golden cup full of milk from her breast – the sacred milk containing *Siva Jnana* (Knowledge of Siva). The child drank the milk, became free from sorrow, and the divine couple disappeared. The child was transformed into an inspired sage, wholly and solely dedicated to Siva. Consequently he received the epithet of *Aludaiya Pillaiyar* ('the God's own child') and *Thiru Jnana Sambandhar* ('he who is conjoined with divine wisdom').

Having drunk the milk of *jnana*, and feeling quite satisfied and happy, Sambandha sat on the tank bund with milk dribbling from the corners of his mouth. When the father came out from his bath, he saw the boy's condition and angrily asked, flourishing a cane, "Who gave you milk? Can you drink milk given by strangers? Tell me who that person is or I will beat you."

Sambandha immediately replied by singing ten Tamil verses. The gist of the first verse is: "The man with *kundalas*

85

(sacred earrings), the Man who rides the sacred bull, the Man who has the white moon on his head, the Man whose body is smeared with the ashes of the burning ghat, the thief who has stolen my heart. He came to bless Brahma, the Creator, when Brahma, with the Vedas in his hand did penance. He who occupies the sacred seat of Brahmapuri, He, my Father, is there, and She, my Mother who gave me milk, is there!" So saying he described the forms of Siva and Parvathi who had given him milk, and also pointed out the temple chariot.

It was clear from the verses, that those who gave milk to the child were no other than Parvathi and Lord Siva. A large gathering of people witnessed this unique scene. From that day onwards, the boy's poetic flow continued unimpeded.

THE LORD IS WITHIN ME

THE MADURA KING Pandyan was inclined towards Jainism. His wife was the daughter of the Chola King and was attached to Saivism. She had heard of the great saint Jnana Sambandar, his powers. And she also came to know of his camping at Vedaranyam. The Pandyan Queen, with the help of a minister who was also attached to *Saivism*, sent an invitation to the Saint to visit Madurai and convert the king to *Saivism*. The Saint came accordingly. When the queen saw that he was a mere boy of about ten or even less, she had serious misgivings whether he could be a match for all the big Jain leaders surrounding the king and if by inviting this child she had put him in jeopardy. When the Saint noticed this, he sang some songs, addressed to the queen and assuring her, "I am not in any way inferior to these Jains. The Lord is within me. Don't, therefore, be afraid."

A devotee added, "The songs mention the names of Jain leaders, referring to them in contempt and stating, 'I am not inferior to all these, as the Lord is within me'. It is amusing to read those songs."

Bhagavan added, "This was after the saint came to Madurai. When the invitation reached Vedaranyam and Jnana Sambandar wanted to start for Madurai, Appar (Tirunavukkarasar) who was with Sambandar pleaded, 'Do not start today. The day is not auspicious for you. They, the Jains, are terrible and powerful persons'. Thereupon Jnana Sambandar sang the *Kolaru Padhikam*, in which he again says, 'As the Lord is within me, in my heart, no days, no planets, can affect me adversely and every day of the week is equally auspicious'."

In the afternoon a copy of *Thevaram* was brought and the above two songs were picked out and Bhagavan read a few of them aloud. In the Madurai hymn Bhagavan referred to the last stanza and said, "When I explained the first stanza in the morning I gave the meaning as 'Because the Lord is within me' though the words only mean 'Because there is the Lord'. I was wondering whether I was justified in my interpretation. I find in the last stanza it is clearly mentioned by the saint himself that what he meant was 'Because the Lord is within me'. Besides, the same is clear from the whole of the *Kolaru padhikam*. Look at the last verse in the Madurai decad. With what authority he sings, 'No harm can approach those who sing these songs of the king of Shiyali (Sirkali) and the Master of Tamil'. Similarly in the last song he says, 'By my order those who read these shall be saved'."

PILGRIMAGE TO
SRI ARUNACHALA

"IN *SRI RAMANA LILA* it is stated that while Sambandha was coming to Tiruvannamalai the forest tribes robbed him of his possessions. He was a man of wisdom and knowledge. What property had he?", asked Suri Nagamma.

"Oh! That! He followed the path of devotion, didn't he? Therefore he had golden bells and a pearl palanquin and other symbols of that nature according to the injunctions of *Iswara*. He also had a *Mutt* (an establishment) and all that a *Mutt* requires," said Bhagavan.

"Is that so? When did he get all those?" Suri Nagamma further enquired.

Bhagavan replied with a voice full of emotion, "From the time when he acquired the name of Jnana Sambandha, that is, even from his childhood, he used to sing with uninterrupted poetic flow and go on pilgrimages. He first visited a holy place called Thirukolakka, went into the temple there and sang verses in praise of the Lord, keeping time with his little hands. By the grace of Siva, cymbals of gold inscribed with the mystic five letters were miraculously put into his hands, and with them he kept time to his songs. Thereafter he visited Chidambaram and other holy places and then went to a pilgrim centre called Maranpadi. There were no trains in those days, you see. The presiding deity in that place observed this little boy visiting holy places on foot. His heart melted with pity, and He created a pearl palanquin, a pearl umbrella and other accompaniments bedecked with pearls suitable for *sannyasis*. He left them in the temple and appeared to the *brahmin* priests and to Sambandha in their dreams, telling the *brahmins*, 'Give them to Sambandha with proper honours,' and told Sambandha, 'The *brahmins* will give you all these; take them.' As they were gifts from Gods he could not refuse them. So Sambandha accepted them with reverential salutations by doing *pradakshina* etc., and then got into the palanquin. From that time onwards, he used to go about in that palanquin wherever he went. Gradually some staff gathered around him and a *Mutt* was established. But whenever he approached a holy place, he used to alight from the palanquin as soon as he saw the *gopuram* (tower) of the shrine and from there onwards, he travelled on foot until he entered the temple. He came here (i.e. Arunachala) on foot from Tirukoilur observing the same principle since, as you know, the peak of Arunagiri is visible from there."

A Tamil devotee said that that visit was not clearly mentioned in *Periapuranam*, to which Bhagavan replied as follows: "No. It is not in *Periapuranam*. But it is stated in Upamanyu's *Sivabhaktivilasam* in Sanskrit. Sambandha worshipped Viratteswara, the presiding deity at Kilur and won the god's favour with his verses and then he worshipped Athulyanatheswara, the presiding deity at Arakandanallur in the same way. From there he beheld the peak of Arunagiri and sang verses out of excess of joy and installed an image of Arunachaleswara in the same spot.

"While he was seated there on a mandapam, God Arunachaleswara appeared to him first in the shape of a *jyoti* (light) and then in the shape of an old *brahmin*. Sambandha did not know who that old *brahmin* was. The *brahmin* had in his hand a flower basket. Unaccountably, Sambandha's mind was attracted towards that *brahmin* like a magnet. He at once asked him with folded hands, 'Where do you come from?' 'I have just come from Arunachalam. My village is here, nearby,' replied the *brahmin*. Sambandha asked him in surprise, 'Arunachala! But how long ago did you come here?' The *brahmin* replied indifferently, 'How long ago? Daily I come here in the morning to gather flowers to make a garland for Lord Arunachala and return there by the afternoon'. Sambandha was surprised and said, 'Is that so? But they said it is very far from here?' The old *brahmin* said, 'Who told you so? You can reach there in one stride. What is there great in it?' Having heard that, Sambandha became anxious to visit Arunachala and asked, 'If so, can I walk there?' The old man replied, 'Ah! If an aged man like me goes there and comes here daily, can't a youth like you do it? What are you saying?' With great eagerness Sambandha asked, 'Sir, if that is so, please take me also along with you,' and started at once with all his entourage. The *brahmin* was going in advance and the party was following behind. Suddenly the *brahmin* disappeared.

"As the party was looking here and there, in confusion, a group of hunters surrounded them, and robbed them of the palanquin, umbrella, golden bells, the pearls and other valuable items, their provisions and even the clothes they were wearing. They were left with only their loin cloths. They did not know the way; it was very hot and there was no shelter, and all were hungry as it was time for taking food. What could they do?

"Then Sambandha prayed to God, 'Oh! Lord, why am I being tested like this? I don't care what happens to me, but why should these followers of mine be put to this hard test?' On hearing those prayers, God appeared in his real form and said, 'My son, these hunters too are my *pramatha ganas* (personal attendants). They deprived you of all your possessions as it is best to proceed to the worship of Lord Arunachala without any show or pomp. All your belongings will be restored to you as soon as you reach there. It is noon time now. You may enjoy the feast and then proceed further'. So saying he disappeared.

"At once, a big tent appeared on a level space nearby. Some *brahmins* came out of the tent and invited Sambandha and his party to their tent, entertained them to a feast with delicious dishes of various kinds and with *chandanam* (sandal paste) and *thambulam* (betel leaves). Sambandha, who was all along entertaining others, was himself entertained by the Lord Himself. After they had rested for a while, one of the *brahmins* in the tent got up and said, 'Sir, shall we proceed to Arunagiri?' Sambandha was extremely happy and accompanied the *brahmin* along with his followers. But as soon as they set out on their journey, the tent together with the people in it disappeared.

"While Sambandha was astonished at the strange happenings, the guide who had been leading them to Arunachala disappeared as soon as they arrived there. Suddenly, the tent along with the people in it and the hunters who had robbed them previously appeared on all sides, and placing before Sambandha all his belongings which they had robbed him of earlier, they vanished. With tears of joy and with a thrill in his body, Sambandha praised the Lord, for His great kindness, stayed there for some days, worshipped Him with flowers of verses in praise of Him and then proceeded on his journey. Out of His affection for Sambandha, who was serving Him with reverence. God Himself, it seems, invited him to this hill.

"Jnana Sambandha thus became one of the most famous *bhaktas* and was much sought after. He led a vigorous and active life and went on pilgrimage to several places in South India. He got married in his sixteenth year. The bride and the bridegroom went to have *darsan* of God in the local temple soon after the marriage ceremonies were over. A large party went with them. When they reached the temple the place was a blaze of light and the temple was not visible. There was however a passage visible in the blaze of light. Jnana Sambandha told the people to enter the passage. He himself went round the light with his young wife, came to the passage and entered it as the others had done earlier. The Light vanished leaving no trace of those who entered it. The temple again came into view as usual. Such was the brief but very eventful life of the sage."

So saying, Bhagavan assumed silence, with his heart filled with devotion and with his voice trembling with emotion.

SAMBANDHAR AND APPAR

WHILE ON A pilgrimage, the twelve-year old Sambandhar and Appar reached Vedaranyam. The main gate of the Vedaranya temple was found locked. It seems that long ago the ancient Vedas took human shapes. They worshipped the Lord in the temple with *abhishekam* (pouring of water) and *puja*. On going away, closed the main gate and sealed it. Since then no one had the courage to open it and so a hole was bored through the wall and a side gate improvised for people for coming and going out. When Appar and Sambandhar enquired about the closure of the main gate, the watchman told them this story and suggested that they could go in by the side gate. They did not feel like using that gate and so decided to pray to *Iswara* for the opening of the main gate. Sambandhar suggested that Appar should pray. It was then that Appar sang a hymn of ten verses. *Iswara* is fond of Appar's songs and it seems He was so absorbed in hearing them, that He forgot to open the gate. When the gate did not open even on singing the ninth verse, Appar was overwhelmed with grief and sang the tenth verse saying, "Oh Lord, has not your heart melted yet?" When even that had no effect, he sang the eleventh verse beginning, *"Avakkanai Vavalaladar Thittaneer"*, the purport of which is, "When Ravana lifted Mt. Kailas with his hands you struck him down with your little finger and inflicted trouble on him for a thousand years. That being so, how will you have compassion for me?" When this was sung, it seems that *Iswara* regretted the delay and immediately opened the doors.

After entering the temple and worshipping the Lord therein, they came out. Appar requested Sambandhar to pray to *Iswara* to close the door and when Sambandhar sang only one verse, the doors closed with a bang. On this occasion, *Iswara* tested Appar by not answering his prayers until he sang eleven songs and favoured Sambandhar by promptly closing the doors when he sang only one song.

On another occasion, it was Sambandhar that was put to a severe test while Appar was readily granted favour. From the time *Iswara* put him to a severe test at Vedaranyam, Appar felt aggrieved and began worshipping *Iswara* with greater devotion than ever. Subsequently both Appar and Sambandhar went on a pilgrimage with their respective retinue and reached a village called Tiruveelimalai. At that time the village was in the grip of a famine. Unable to bear the sight of the sufferings of the people they decided to stay in two different *Mutts* along with their attendants and distribute food to the people. They had of course no money with them and so went to the local temple to pray to *Iswara*. Pleased with their devotion, *Iswara* gave them a sovereign each every day. The sovereign used to be kept on the doorstep. The one given to Appar was accepted by the vendors of foodstuffs and the required articles were readily supplied. Food could therefore be given to the people before the afternoon set in. The sovereign of Sambandhar was however below the standard purity of gold and so the dealers offered to take it only at a discount. The attendants had therefore to come back to the *Mutt* to obtain Sambandhar's consent, then return to the shop, buy the required articles and then feed the people rather late, by about 2 P.M. everyday.

In due course this delay came to the notice of Sambandhar. On enquiry he found that it was all due to the bad coins he was getting from the Lord daily. He went to the temple and sang ten songs beginning with "*Vachiteerave Kachunalguveer*", which means, "Swami, why are you giving me coins which are not pure gold?" Then the Lord who is the embodiment of kindness, said, "Appar is worshipping me with his mind, speech and deed, while you are doing it with your mind and speech only". Appar was daily cleaning the temple grounds, making them neat and tidy. "It was only to point out the difference that I have been doing like this. Henceforth, I shall give you also good coins. Don't worry". And from that day onwards good coins were given.

SAINT APPAR

APPAR WAS BORN in a village called Tiruvamur in the Thirumunaipadi region of a Vellala family of Saivaites. His father's name was Pugazhanar and mother's name was Madiniyar. His parents named him Marul Neekkiyar. He had only one sister by name Tilakavati. As he grew up he became proficient in all branches of knowledge. When Tilakavati was 12 years of age, the parents decided to give her in marriage to a commander in the king's army. Just then there was a war and that commander went away saying he would marry her on his return. In the meantime Pugazhanar passed away and his wife Madiniyar committed *Sati*. The brother and sister were left alone. They awaited the return of the commander, but after some time they heard that the commander had died in the war. Tilakavati wanted to commit *Sati* as her parents had decided to give her away in marriage to that commander and she felt that her body was therefore his. Marul Neekkiyar with great grief, fell at the feet of his sister and told her that he looked up to her as his father and mother, and if she insisted on dying on the funeral pyre, he would also commit suicide. As she was anxious that her brother should live and prosper, she gave up her idea of committing *Sati*. She however did not marry but remained at home absorbed in the service of the Siva temple and in her own *tapas* (austerity).

Marul Neekkiyar realised that material wealth was transitory. Whatever money, gold and other valuables he had, he gave away, became a *sannyasi*, left home and in his wanderings reached Patalipuram (Tiruppadiripuliyur, i.e. Cuddalore). The most important place at that time was the Samana *Mutt*. As fate would have it, he went there and joined the Samana cult (a Jain

97

cult), was given the title of Darmasena, and became the Head of the *Mutt*, the *Purohit* of the Raja and the Poet Laureate of the kingdom. He therefore stayed on there.

Tilakavathi, who was staying at her native place, heard this news and felt sad. She went to their family deity, Veerasthaneswara, on the banks of the river Gedila and prayed to God several times to save her brother from following the ways of the heretics. One day Parameswara appeared to her in a dream and said, "O *Tapaswini*, you can now give up your mental agony. In his last birth, your brother was a *sannyasi*, but did not perform *tapas* properly. There was a flaw in his *tapas*. As a result of that, he has now joined that heretic (*Pashanda*) cult. I shall now save him by making him suffer from stomach ache. Give up your grief and relax."

Immediately thereafter, Dharmasena had a violent stomach ache. Several people in that *Mutt* who were well versed in *mantras* and *tantras* tried their best to cure him but could not succeed and so gave up all hopes. Dharmasena could not bear the agony any longer. He then remembered his sister. Hoping she might be of some help, he sent a man to fetch her. She refused to give up her own *dharma* and go to the Samana *Mutt*. On hearing that, Dharmasena regretted his having given up his own *dharma*, namely *Saivism*, and without the knowledge of other people in the *Mutt*, left the *Mutt* at night, with two servants for his native place. When he tapped at the door and called his sister, she recognised his voice and opened the door. He fell at her feet and requested her to forgive him. She received him with open arms and overjoyed at the kindness of Parameswara, and after giving him holy ash, taught her brother the *Panchakshari Mantra*. He smeared the holy ash all over his body and repeated the *mantra*.

Tilakavati took her brother to the temple of Veerasthaneswara. When he prostrated and got up, Marul Neekkiyar began composing songs in Tamil in praise of Siva. The first of the Ten Verses (*Padikam*) begins with '*Kootrayinavaru*'. His stomach ache ceased immediately. That is why there is a belief that whoever recites these songs gets relief from all illness.

After that, he took up *Sannyasa* and went on a pilgrimage singing his *Padikams* (containing 10 verses each). In due course he reached Chidambaram. After worshipping Nataraja there, and singing the *Padikams*, he went with his followers to nearby Sirkali. He had heard that Sambandar had become a saint by drinking the milk of the mother of the universe, Parvati, when he was a little child. Hearing that he was coming, Sambandar with his followers went out to meet him. As soon as they met, Marul Neekkiyar fell at the feet of Sambandar. The latter lifted him up with his hands with great affection, and as a show of respect, called him 'Appah'. Appar immediately claimed that he was the *Dasan* (servant) of Sambandar. From that time onwards, Marul Neekkiyar came to be known as Appar. Subsequently both of them went together to the temple of Brahmapureeswara. Sambandar then asked Appar to worship the Lord, which Appar did with his *Padikams*. After that, they went together to several temples and sang *Padikams* in praise of the Lord. You have already heard of Vedaranyam and the sovereigns. There are several other stories like that. After his contact with Appar, Sambandar went to Patalipuram, defeated the people of Samana *Mutt* by arguments and established *Saivism*. They always used to be together.

THERE IS NOTHING WITHOUT

Umadevi, a Polish lady had travelled in Kashmir and brought some photos which were shown to all in the old hall. Bhagavan humorously remarked, "We have seen those places without the trouble of travelling." A devotee thereby said, "I wish to go to Kailas."

Sri Bhagavan said, "One can see these places only if destined. Not otherwise. After seeing all, there will still remain more — if not in this hemisphere, may be in the other. Knowledge implies ignorance of what lies beyond what is known. Knowledge is always limited." After sometime Sri Bhagavan related the following story.

APPAR WAS DECREPIT and old and yet began to a travel to Kailas. Another old man appeared on the way and tried to dissuade him from the attempt, saying that it was too difficult to reach there. Appar was however obdurate and said that he would risk his life in the attempt. The stranger asked him to dip himself in a tank close by. Appar did so and found Kailas then and there. Where did all this happen? In Tiruvayyar, nine miles from Tanjore. Where is Kailas then? Is it within the mind or outside it? If Tiruvayyar be truly Kailas, it must appear to others as well. But Appar alone found it so.

Similarly it is said of other places of pilgrimage in the South, that they are the abodes of Siva, and devotees found them so. This was true from their standpoint. Everything is within. There is nothing without.

WITH THE MOON IN HIS CROWN

THE VENERABLE SUNDARAMURTHY was born in the *amsa* of Aalaala Sundara, who emanated from the reflection of Lord Siva, the Somasekhara (with moon in his crown). He acquired the friendship of the Kerala king, Cheraman Perumal Nainar, in the course of his wanderings as a pilgrim, and together they both went to Madurai on pilgrimage. The Pandyan king as well as his son-in-law, the Chola king, extended a very warm welcome to them and expressed their happiness at being their hosts. Sundaramurthy worshipped God Sundareswara, the consort of the goddess Meenakshi, and sang hymns in praise of the Lord with his poetic skill. Accompanied by the Chera king he visited and worshipped at the sacred shrines of the south, namely Thirukuttralam, Tirunelveli and Rameswaram. From there he visited the sacred shrine of Thirukkedeswara in Lanka Dwipa (Ceylon) and offered worship. There he remembered Thrisulapuram (Thiruchuli) which is the Muktinagar (city of salvation) and proceeded thither. As they approached that city, the crowds saw them both resplendent as though the sun and the moon appeared at the same time. Sundaramurthy was happy to have the *darsan* of Lord Bhuminatha and offered worship with the song beginning '*Oona uyir Puhalai*' and was overwhelmed with devotion. He decided to stay in that holy place for a while, and resided in the *Mutt* on the bank of the river Kowndinya.

One night during his stay there, Lord Siva appeared to him in a dream with a ball in his hand (ball is the symbol of

101

kingship) and a crown on his head, as a youth of incomparable beauty. With a smile dancing on his lips, he said, "We stay in *Jyotivana* (Kaleswara)." On hearing these words, Sundaramurthy woke up with excitement and recollected the glorious kindness of the Lord who appeared and showered benevolence on him, and narrated the wonderful vision to the Chera king with joy. There and then he sang, overwhelmed with devotion, the *Thevara Pathikam* commencing with the words, '*Thondar Adithodalalum*' on Lord Kaleswara.

From there they started to visit the far off holy place, Thiruppunavayil. Even as they started, God Kaleswara (who appeared in the dream of Sundaramurthy) and Amba approached them in the guise of an old *brahmin* couple. When Sundaramurthy asked them, "Who are you? Where do you come from?" they replied, "We shall talk about that later. First give us food. We are hungry." Sundaramurthy consented, got the food prepared and looked for the couple, but they were not to be seen anywhere. All the lanes and by-lanes of the village were searched but they could not be found anywhere. They came back to the *Mutt* only to find that the food had disappeared and the leaves in which the food was eaten were scattered all over the place. Sundaramurthy was wonder-struck and exclaimed, "Ah! What a wonder is this! What can this be except the *leela* (play) of the Lord of the Universe?" As he arrived at this conclusion he heard an invisible voice: "Where do you intend going without seeing us who reside in the *Jyotivana?*" Sundaramurthy was wondering where that *Jyotivana* was and how to go there. The invisible voice once again said, "We are proceeding there on the vehicle of the sacred bull Nandi. You may also come there, following its footsteps."

Sundaramurthy followed the footsteps, accompanied by the devotees, but suddenly the track disappeared. As he stood there in confusion the invisible voice was heard to say, "Look carefully". As he followed carefully the footsteps he saw a particular place full of *Siva Lingas*. There was no space even for a single step forward and he and the other devotees stood there bewildered. Suddenly he saw a narrow footpath and they went along it, on and on until at last they beheld the temple of Kaleswara. They all took their bath in the tank in front of the temple, and as they were thinking of going into the temple, all of a sudden the temple with its tower disappeared. Sundaramurthy was wonder-struck and sang some songs in praise of the Lord, conveying the idea: "Is this the result of my not having come for worship in your temple before bathing?" At once a whole view of *jyoti* (light) appeared and the peak view of a temple tower and then the temple itself with its compound wall. He was overjoyed, had a *darsan* of God, worshipped Him, sang songs in praise of Him, and then proceeded on his pilgrimage. This is a wonderful story. There are many more stories of him.

SWAMI IS EVERYWHERE

An American lady unaccustomed to squatting on the floor, somehow managed to sit in the hall by stretching her legs towards Bhagavan's sofa. One of the attendants suggested to her that she sit cross-legged. When Bhagavan saw that, he said smiling, "When they find it difficult even to sit down on the floor, should you force them to sit cross-legged also?" "No, no! As they do not know that it is disrespectful to stretch their legs towards Bhagavan, I merely told them so, that is all," said the devotee. "Oh is that so! It is disrespectful, is it? Then it is disrespectful for me to stretch my legs towards them. What you say applies to me as well." Saying this in a lighter vein, Bhagavan sat up cross-legged. Even though the rheumatism in Bhagavan's legs rendered them painful and stiff after ten minutes of being folded, he continued to sit cross-legged stretching them from time to time, saying that it might be deemed disrespectful. Even after the visitors took leave he kept his legs folded saying, "I do not know if I can stretch them. They say it is not good manners." The attendant stood by Bhagavan's side crestfallen and repentant. Bhagavan, full of compassion, stretched out his legs as usual and began telling this story.

SEEING THAT SUNDARAMURTHI was going away on a white elephant which had come from Kailas, the Rajah of Chera whispered in the ear of his horse the *panchakshara mantra* and got upon it to go to Kailas. Avvaiyar, who was at the time doing *puja* to Lord Ganesa, saw them both going to Kailas and so tried to hurry up her *puja* as she too wanted to go to Kailas. Seeing that, Ganesa said, "Old woman, don't hurry. Let your *puja* be performed as usual. I shall take you to Kailas before they reach it." Accordingly, the *puja* was performed in due course. Waving his hand around, he said, "Old lady, close your eyes." That was all. When she opened her eyes, she found herself seated in Kailas in front of Parvati and Parameswara. By the time Sundaramurthi and Chera Raja reached the place, they found her already seated there. Surprised at that, they asked her how she had got there and were overjoyed at her *bhakti*.

After all, she was very old. So she sat facing Parameswara with her legs stretched out like me. Parvati could not bear that sight. She was worried because to sit with legs stretched out towards Swami, she felt, was a great insult. She respectfully suggested to Parameswara that she should be permitted to tell the old lady about it. "Oh, don't speak, don't open your mouth. We should not say anything to her." How could Parvati put up with that insult? She therefore whispered into the ear of her maid to tell the old lady, who said, "Grandma, Grandma, don't keep your legs outstretched towards *Iswara*". "Is that so?" She replied, "Tell me on which side *Iswara* is not present. Shall I turn this side?" asked Avvaiyar. So saying, she turned her outstretched legs to another side and *Iswara* got turned to that side; and when again she turned to a different direction, He also got turned to the same side. Thus Swami got turned to whichever side she turned her legs. Looking at Parvati, *Iswara* said, "Do you see now? You would not listen to me. See how she turns me this side and that. That is why I told you not to open your mouth." Then Parvati requested the old lady to excuse her. It is similar to that when people are asked not to stretch their legs towards *Swami*. Where is He not present?

SUNDARAMURTHI'S BOND
OF SERVITUDE

SUNDARAMURTHY WAS BORN in the sacred place Tirunavalur in Thirumunaippadi region in the Siva Brahmana caste called *Adi Saivam*, to a Siva priest named Chadayanar alias Sivacharya and his wife Isaijnaniyar. He was named by his parents Nambiyarurar. One day, while he was playing in the street with a toy cart, the king of the place, by name Narasinga Muniyar, saw him and took a fancy to him. He requested the father, Sivacharya to let him have the boy. The father agreed and the boy was brought up by the king as his foster son. Even so, the *brahminical* usages regarding thread ceremony and *vedic* instructions were carefully observed and he became well-versed in all the arts.

When he came of age, his marriage with the daughter of a relative by name Chatangavi Sivacharya was decided upon, and invitations were issued to all relatives for the function. Sundaramurthy went through the usual premarital ceremonies a day before the marriage, and on the marriage day, properly dressed as the bridegroom accompanied by his relatives, he went to the bride's father's house in Puttur village, quite early in the morning on horseback. On reaching the bride's house, he alighted from the horse and sat on the wedding seat in the marriage *pandal* in accordance with the usual custom. Drums were sounded and the arrival of the bride was awaited.

Just then, Lord Siva approached the marriage *pandal* in the garb of an old *brahmin*, and announced, "All of you please listen to what I have to say." On their assenting, the old man told the boy, "Look here, there is an agreement between you and me. First fulfil it and then marry." The boy replied, "If there is an agreement, let it be so, but tell us first what it is." The old *brahmin* told the audience, "Sirs, this boy is my servant. I have with me the deed of service executed by his grandfather in my favour." Sundaramurthy replied, "Oh! Madman, Enough! We are hearing for the first time that a *brahmin* is the servant of another *brahmin*. Go, get away!" The *brahmin* replied, "I am neither a mad man nor a devil. I am not offended at your remarks. You have not understood me at all. Stop this childish talk and come and serve me." Sundaramurthy then said, "Show me the deed." "Who are you to decide after seeing the deed?" said the old man. "If the people in the audience see the deed and agree that it is true, you should begin to serve me." Sundaramurthy got very angry and pounced upon the man to snatch the deed from him. The *brahmin* ran away, but the boy pursued him, snatched the deed at last, and tore it to pieces. The old man caught hold of Sundaramurthy and began shouting. The marriage guests got agitated over that, separated the two and said to the *brahmin*, "You are speaking of arrangements unheard of in this world. Oh! Quarrelsome old man! Where do you come from?" The *brahmin* replied, "I belong to the village of Thiruvennainallur. Don't you agree that this boy Nambiyarurar has confirmed his servitude to me by unjustly snatching away the service deed from my hands and tearing it to pieces?" Sundarar replied, "If indeed you are a resident of Thiruvennainallur village, your claim can be decided there, can't it be?" The *brahmin* replied, "Yes. Come with me. I shall produce the original deed before the Council of *brahmins* there and establish my claim that you are my servant." Accordingly the *brahmin* walked ahead and Sundaramurthy and all the other *brahmins* followed him.

As soon as they all reached the Council of *brahmins* in the other village, the cunning old *brahmin* filed his claim petition before them to the effect that the boy Nambiyarurar tore up the service deed in his favour. The councillors said, "We have not heard anywhere in this world that *brahmins* become servants of *brahmins*." The *brahmin* replied, "No. Mine is not a false claim. The deed that this boy tore up is the deed of service executed by his grandfather to be my servants." The councillors asked Sundaramurthy, "Can you win your case by merely tearing up the deed executed by your grandfather? What do you say?" He replied, "Oh virtuous men, learned in all the vedic lore! You all know that I am an *Adi Saiva*. Even if this old *brahmin* is able to establish that I am his servant, you must please consider it a piece of magic beyond the reach of mental reasoning. What can I say of such a claim?" The councillors told the *brahmin*, "You must first prove to us that he is your servant. To decide an affair of this nature, three things are needed – custom, written evidence and oral evidence. Should you not produce at least one of these three items?" The *brahmin* replied, "Sir! What he tore up is only the duplicate copy; the original deed is with me." The councillors demanded the production of the original deed, and gave him an assurance that it would not be torn up by Sundaramurthy. The old man took out the original deed from the folds of the cloth around his waist, and showed it to them. The village *Karnam* who happened to come there unexpectedly then, was asked to read it. He bowed before the councillors, opened the folds of the original document and so as to be heard by all, he read it out aloud as follows: 'I, *Adi Saiva* by caste and Arurar by name, residing in Thiruvennainallur village have executed this deed of service gladly and out of my own free will, undertaking to do service by me and by my successive descendants, to *Pitthan* (mad man) residing in Thiruvennainallur village. (Sd.) Arurar."

The witness to the deed were those very councillors and they all identified and confirmed that the signatures were their own. The councillors asked Sundaramurthy to verify if the handwriting in the deed was his grandfather's.

The man pretending to be a *brahmin* said, "Sir! This is a mere boy. How can he identify his grandfather's writing? If there is any other paper available containing his grandfather's writing, please send for it and compare." They all agreed, and the relatives of Sundaramurthy searched, and produced a paper containing his grandfather's handwriting. The councillors compared the two papers and confirmed that the writings in the two papers were identical. They told Sundaramurthy, "Boy! There is no way of escape for you. You have lost. It is your duty to do service according to this old man's orders." Sundaramurthy was stupefied at this and said that he would obey the order, if fate had decreed that way.

They had compassion on the boy, and had still some doubts about the *brahmin*, and questioned him, "Sir! This deed says that you belong to this very village. Can you show us where your ancestral house and property and all that are?" The *brahmin* pretended surprise, and said, "What! You are all of this village, so learned, so intelligent, so elderly – does not even one among you know my house? How surprising are your words! Come with me then!" So saying, he led the way, and they all followed. They saw the *brahmin* enter Siva's temple called 'Thiruvarul Thurai', and they were stupefied.

Sundaramurthy thought, "The *brahmin* who made me his servant has entered the temple of my God Parameswara! What a wonder!" So thinking, he followed alone eagerly the footsteps of the *brahmin* and entered the temple with great desire and shouted, "Oh *brahmin*!" At once Lord Siva appeared in the company of Goddess Parvathi, seated on the sacred bull, and said, "My son! You are Aalaala Sundara, one of my *pramatha ganas* (chief attendants). You were born here as a result of a curse. You requested me to have you as My own, wherever you might be, even during the period of the curse. I therefore made you my servant here."

109

As soon as Sundaramurthy heard those words of the Great Lord he was overjoyed like the calf that heard the mother-cow's call. With his voice trembling with emotion and eyes filled with tears of joy, he made prostrations to Him, and with folded hands said, "Oh Lord! You are gracious to my worthless self, hold me fast to you like the cat holding on to its kitten, and make me your own. What gracious kindness!", and praised Him. The Great Lord was pleased and said, "My son! Because you have disputed with me, you shall have the name of '*Van Thondan*'. The service to be rendered hereafter by you to me, is to worship me with flowers of verses. Compose verses on me and sing them."

With folded hands, Sundaramurthy said, "Oh Lord! You came in the guise of a *brahmin* and preferred a claim against me, and I contested and argued with you, not knowing your greatness. You are the great Lord that gave me recollection of my past and saved me from falling into worldly actions and behaviour and getting drowned therein. What do I know of your limitless great qualities, and what shall I sing of them?" *Iswara* said, "You already called me *Pithan*, mad man. Therefore, sing of me as the Mad Man." So saying, he disappeared. Sundaramurthy immediately sang the *Sri Padikam*, commencing with the verse: '*Pittha pirai sudi*'."

MANIKKAVACHAKAR

MANIKKAVACHAKAR WAS BORN in a village called Vaadavur (Vaatapuri) in Pandya *Desa*. Because of that people used to call him Vaadavurar. He was sent to school very early. He read religious books, absorbed the lessons therein, and became noted for his devotion to Siva, as also his kindness to living beings. Having heard about him, the Pandya king sent for him, made him his Prime Minister and conferred on him the title of "*Thennavan Brahmarayan*" i.e., Leader among *brahmins* in the south. Though he performed the duties of a minister with tact and integrity, he had no desire for material happiness. His mind was always absorbed in spiritual matters. Feeling convinced that for the attainment of *jnana*, the grace of the guru is essential, he kept on making enquiries about it.

Once the Pandya king directed the minister to buy a few good horses and bring them to him. As he was already in search of a guru, Manikkavachakar felt that it was a good opportunity and started with his retinue, carrying with him the required amount of gold. He visited all the temples on the way and reached a village called Tiruperundurai. For about a year before that, Parameswara had assumed the form of a school teacher and was teaching the poor children of the village seated on a street pial, near the temple. He had his meal which consisted of only cooked green vegetables, in the house of his pupils everyday by turn. Well aware of the mental maturity of Manikkavachakar, *Iswara* anxiously awaited his arrival. By the time Manikkavachakar came, *Iswara* assumed the form of a *Siddha Purusha* (realised soul) and sat under a *Kurundai* (yellow amanth) tree within the temple. Many *sannyasis* had gathered around him. Manikkavachakar came

111

to the temple, had *darsan* of the Lord in the sanctum sanctorum, and while doing *pradakshina* around the temple, saw the *Siddha Purusha*. He was thrilled at the sight and tears welled up in his eyes. Spontaneously, he lifted his hands above his head in salutation and prostrated at the feet of *Iswara*. He then got up, and prayed that he, a humble being, may also be accepted as a disciple. Having come to earth solely to bestow grace on Manikkavachakar, *Iswara*, through His mere look, gave him *jnana upadesa* (initiation into knowledge). Manikkavachakar felt indescribable happiness and the *upadesa* given by *Iswara* took deep root in his heart. With folded hands and tears of joy, Manikkavachakar went round the guru, offered salutations, stripped himself of all his official dress and ornaments, placed them near the guru and stood before him with only a *kowpeenam* on. A deeply felt inspiration resulted in his spontaneously composing and singing beautiful and moving devotional songs in praise of his guru. *Iswara* was pleased, and addressing him as 'Manikkavachaka', commanded him to remain there, worshipping Him and singing His praise. His mission fulfilled, the Lord disappeared.

Fully convinced that he who had blessed him was no other than *Iswara* Himself, Manikkavachakar was stricken with unbearable grief and fell on the ground weeping and saying, "Oh! My lord, Why did you go away leaving me here?" The villagers were very much surprised at this and began a search for the person who was till then working in their village as a schoolteacher but could not find him anywhere. Then they realised that it was the Lord's *leela*. Some time later, Manikkavachakar got over his grief, decided to act according to the injunctions of *Iswara*, sent away his retinue to Madurai, spent all the gold with him on the temple and stayed there alone.

Hearing all that had happened, the king immediately sent an order to Manikkavachakar to return to Madurai, but then how could he go to the king without the horses?

If he wanted to purchase them, where was the money? Not knowing what to do, he prayed to Lord Siva for help. That night Lord Siva appeared to him in a dream, gave him a priceless gem and said, "Give this to the king and tell him the horses will come on the day of the *Moola* star in the month of *Sravana*". Startled at that vision he opened his eyes but the Lord was not there. Manikkavachakar was however, overjoyed at what had happened, put on his official dress and went to Madurai. He gave the gem to the king, discussed the auspicious time when the horses would be arriving and then anxiously waited for the day. He did not however, resume his official duties. Though his body was in Madurai, his mind was in Tirupperundurai. He was merely biding time. The Pandyan king, however, sent his spies to Perundurai and found out that there were no horses there meant for the king and that all the money meant for their purchase had been spent in the renovation of the temple. So he immediately imprisoned Manikkavachakar making him undergo all the trials and tribulations of prison life.

Meanwhile, as originally arranged, on the day of the *Moola* star, *Iswara* assumed the guise of a horseman transformed the jackals of the jungle into horses, and brought them to the king. The king was astonished at this, took delivery of the horses and according to the advice of the keeper of the stables, had them tied up at the same place where all his other horses were kept. He thanked the horseman profusely and after sending him away with several presents, released Manikkavachakar from prison with profuse apologies. The same night, the new horses changed into their original forms, killed all the horses in the stables, ate them, created similar havoc in the city and fled. The king grew very angry, branded Manikkavachakar a trickster and put him back into prison. Soon, in accordance with *Iswara's* orders, the waters of the river Vaigai rose in floods and the whole of the city of Madurai was under water. Alarmed at that, the king assembled all the people and ordered them to put up bunds around the river. For that purpose, he ordered every citizen to do a certain amount of work with the threat of dire consequences, should they fail to do their allotted work.

There was in Madurai an old woman by name 'Pittuvani Ammaiyar'. She was a pious devotee of Lord Siva. She was living alone earning her livelihood by daily preparing and selling '*Pittu*' (*Pittu* is sweetened powdered rice pressed into conical shapes). She had no one to do her allotted work on the river bund nor had she the money to hire a person to do it. She was therefore greatly worried and cried. "*Iswara*! What shall I do?" Seeing her helplessness, *Iswara* came there in the guise of a coolie, with a spade on his shoulder, and called out, "Granny, granny, do you want a coolie?" "Yes", she said, "But I do not have even a paisa in my hand to pay you. What to do?" He said, "I do not want any money and would be satisfied if you gave me a little *Pittu* to eat. I shall then do the allotted work on the river bund."

Pleased with that offer, she began making *Pittu*, but they did not come out in full shape but were broken. Surprised at this she gave all the bits to the coolie. He ate as many of them as he could and went away saying that he would attend to the bund-raising work. Surprisingly, the dough with the old woman remained intact even though she had prepared and given bits of the *Pittu* to the coolie. The coolie went to the work-spot but instead of doing the work lay down there idly coming in the way of others doing their work.

The king went round to inspect the progress of the work and found that the portion allotted to Ammaiyar remained unattended to. On enquiry, his servants told him all about the pranks of that coolie. The king got infuriated, called the coolie and said, "Instead of doing the allotted work, you are lying down and singing". So saying, he hit the coolie on the back

114

with a cane he had in his hand. The hit not only recoiled on the king himself, but on all living beings there, and all of them suffered the pain on that account. The king immediately realised that the person hit by him was *Parameswara* Himself in the guise of a coolie. The king stood aghast. *Parameswara* vanished and soon a voice from the sky said, "Oh king! Manikkavachakar is my beloved devotee. I myself did all this to show you his greatness. Release him and seek his blessings."

Soon after hearing that voice, the king went to see Manikkavachakar and on the way, he stepped into the house of Pittuvani Ammaiyar to see her. By that time she had already got into a *vimanam* (a heavenly car moving through the skies) and was on her way to Kailas. The king was greatly surprised and saluted her and from there he went straight to Manikkavachakar and fell at his feet. Manikkavachakar lifted him with great respect, and enquired of his welfare. The king said, "Please forgive me and rule this kingdom yourself." Manikkavachakar, looking at the king, said with kindness, "*Appah!* (a term of endearment) As I have already agreed to serve the Lord, I cannot be bothered with the problems of ruling a kingdom. Please do not mistake me. Rule the kingdom yourself looking after the welfare of the people. Henceforth you will have nothing to worry about."

So saying, smilingly, he put on the dress of a *sannyasin* and went about visiting holy places singing the praise of Siva.

How the *Tiruvachakam* was Written

MANIKKAVACHAKAR WAS GOING from one place to another until he came to Chidambaram. While witnessing Nataraja's dance he started singing heart-melting songs and stayed in that place itself. Then one day Nataraja, with a view to make people know the greatness of Manikkavachakar and to bless the people with an excellent collection of hymns, went to the house of Manikkavachakar in the night, in the guise of a *brahmin*. He was received cordially and when asked the purpose of the visit, the Lord smilingly and with great familiarity asked, "It seems you have been singing hymns during your visit to sacred places of pilgrimage and that you are doing it here also. May I hear them? I have been thinking of coming and listening to you for a very long time but could not find the required leisure. That is why I have come here at night. I suppose you don't mind. Can you sing? Do you remember them all?" "There is no need to worry about sleep. I shall sing all the songs I remember. Please listen." So saying Manikkavachakar began singing in ecstasy. The Lord in the guise of a *brahmin* sat down there writing the songs on palm leaves. As Manikkavachakar was in ecstasy he hardly noticed the *brahmin* who was taking down the songs. Singing on and on, he completely forgot himself in the thought of God and ultimately became silent. The old *brahmin* quietly disappeared.

At daybreak, the *dikshitar* (priest) came to the Nataraja temple as usual to perform the morning *puja* and as he opened the doors he found in front of the Nataraja image, on the doorstep, a palm-leaf book. When the book was opened, and scrutinised the words *Tiruvachakam* were written as well as an explanation that the book was written, as dictated by Manikkavachakar. It was signed below *Tiruchitrambalam*, i.e. Chidambaram. The stamp of Sri Nataraja was also there below the signature. Thereupon, all the temple priests gathered in great surprise and sent word to Manikkavachakar, showed him the *Tiruvachakam*, and the signature of Nataraja and asked him to tell them about the genesis of the hymns.

Manikkavachakar did not say anything but asked them to accompany him, went to the temple of Nataraja and standing opposite the Lord said, "Sirs, the Lord in front of us is the only answer to your question. He is the answer." After having said that, he merged into the Lord.

As he narrated the story, Bhagavan's voice got choked. Unable to speak any more he remained in ecstatic silence.

Yoga Vasishtam

Yoga Vasishta is a dialogue between Sage Vasishta and Sri Rama during which *advaita* is expounded illustrated profusely with stories. Sri Bhagavan referred to *Yoga Vasishta* frequently and has even incorporated nine verses from it, in his *Supplement to Forty Verses*.

BRAHMA, THE CREATOR

In the course of a conversation a devotee queried, "In
Vasishtam *it is stated that everything comes upon a person*
by the desires of the mind and that it is the mind that creates
them all. But how is it possible, Bhagavan?"

"You ask how! Is this not stated in the story about the
ten brahmins? *That story is also in the* Vasishtam," *said*
Bhagavan. When asked about it, Sri Bhagavan cheerfully
began telling the devotees the story.

ONCE UPON A time Brahma, the creator, after performing
his duties the whole day, went to sleep at nightfall. When the
night was over, he woke up. After completing his morning
ablutions, he looked at the sky before beginning his day's work
of creation, and he saw that there were several other worlds.
His work of creation was being performed properly so there
was no justification for the other worlds to come into existence.
"What! The worlds that should remain dormant until I created
them have come into existence! How have these worlds come
into existence?" Greatly surprised at this, with the power of his
mind he summoned one of the suns in those worlds and asked
"Sir, how have these worlds come into existence?"

The sun replied, "Oh, my Lord, you are the Brahma.
What is there that you do not know? Even so, if you want to
hear from me, I will tell you." So saying, he began relating as
follows: "Swami, a *brahmin* living in a city under Mount Kailas,
with his wife prayed to *Parameswara* for children as he had
none. In course of time they begot ten children. The children

in due course grew up and studied the *Sastras*. After some time, the parents passed away and the boys were filled with grief. They had no near relatives and consequently could not continue to live in that house. They climbed Mount Kailas and decided to do *tapas* there. They then began considering what exactly they should do to get rid of their sorrows. At first they thought wealth would give them happiness but dismissed the idea as there would always be wealthier people than them. It would be the same thing with regard to kingship or even the Lordship of *Mahendra*. They therefore felt that there was no fulfilment in any of those things. Finally the eldest amongst them said, 'He who creates all these is Brahma and so Brahma is the greatest of them all.' They all felt happy at the suggestion and said, 'What is the way to achieve Brahma-hood (*Brahmatvam*)?' After thinking for a while, the eldest said, 'It is not so difficult. Mind is the basic cause of everything. So let us all sit in a lonely place and practice concentration for attaining *Brahmatvam*, giving up thoughts on all other matters, including the body. Continuously feel that you are seated on a lotus, that you are lustrous and that you are creating this world and destroying it. I will also do likewise.' All of them felt happy at the idea 'I am Brahma with four faces.' The idea became firmly fixed in their minds and they forgot completely about their bodies. Subsequently those bodies fell off like dry leaves from a tree. On account of the intensity of their desires ten worlds have come into existence as all the ten of them have become Brahmas. The force of their desires is now stationary in the *Chit akasa*. I am the sun of one of the ten worlds." So saying, the sun went back to his original place.

THE CHARM OF
SELF-REALISATION

A Swiss lady: Does Self-realisation imply occult powers also?

M: The Self is the most intimate and eternal Being whereas the siddhis are foreign. The latter requires effort to acquire while the former does not.

The powers are sought by the mind which must be kept alert, whereas the Self is realised when the mind is destroyed. These powers may be sought and gained even after Self-realisation. But then they are used for a definite purpose, i.e. the benefit of others as in the case of Chudala.

KING SIKIDVAJA AND Queen Chudala ruled the kingdom of Malava. Chudala regularly practised meditation in the silent hours. In due course she realised the Absolute Truth and her face shone brightly and became much more beautiful than before. The king observing this asked her the reason. The queen replied that it was due to her realisation of Truth. The king laughed at her, thinking that realisation was possible only through severe austerities and could never be gained while living in a palace. He wanted to leave the kingdom and practise *tapas* in the forest so that he could gain Realisation. The queen tried to dissuade him and suggested that he could carry on the *tapas* in the palace itself and rule the kingdom as well. Refusing to act on her advice, he went to the forest and performed hard penance. The queen was ruling the kingdom in the king's absence.

The queen taking pity on her husband and anxious to rescue him from the mire of delusion, practised *siddhis* and took the guise of one Kumbha Muni and stood in front of him, but a few feet above the ground! The king, thinking that some celestial being had descended from the heavens to bless him, fell at his feet, told him his woes and sought guidance. The *Muni* taught the king as follows: "*Karmas* can give fruit as ordained by the Lord but *karmas* in themselves cannot grant you salvation. By doing disinterested actions, one's mind can become pure. With a pure mind one should contemplate on the Self. This would destroy the *vasanas*. Then one should approach a master and through his grace learn how to enquire into the nature of the Self. Liberation is possible only through enquiry and not by performing any amount of *karma*. By renouncing everything one would realise the Truth."

The king said that he had renounced everything, including his kingdom and family. Kumbha Muni told him that his renunciation was only external and the seeds of attachment were still in him. The king then took out his walking staff, *kamandalu*, *rudrakshas* and clothes and threw them all into the fire and stood without any possession. Still, on being told that he had not renounced completely, the king was ready to drop his last possession, the body, by jumping from the top of the mountain. The *Muni* asked him, "What harm has the body done to deserve the punishment?" Thereby the *Muni* taught him that he would not realise the Truth by destroying the body, but only by destroying the mind which was the source of all attachment. The mind identifies itself as 'I' and this was bondage. The snapping of this identity was renunciation of everything. Then the *Muni* described in detail the *sadhana* of discrimination.

Thus the king's doubts were dispelled and his mind became pure. The king enquired into the source of Self and soon became one with it and remained in blissful *samadhi*. Kumbha Muni disappeared and returned after some time. The king was still in *samadhi*. Chudala roared like a lion to wake him up, but could not. Then taking a subtle form she entered into the king's heart and found it pure and devoid of any latent tendencies. Then in a melodious voice she chanted the *Sama Veda* and like the blossoming of a lotus, the king became aware of the world. The king filled with joy, remained silent not knowing how to express his gratitude. Then as advised by the queen, he returned with her to the kingdom. Thus established in Truth he ruled the kingdom and lived happily with the queen for a long time.

ALMS FOR A KING

IN *VASISHTAM*, THERE is a story about Bhagiratha, before he brought the Ganges down to the earth. He was an emperor but the empire seemed to him a great burden because of *Atmajignasa* (Self-enquiry). In accordance with the advice of his guru and on the pretext of a *Yagna* (sacrifice), he gave away all his wealth and other possessions. No one would, however take the empire. So he invited the neighbouring king who was an enemy and who was waiting for a suitable opportunity and gifted away the empire to him. The only thing that remained to be done was leaving the country. He left at midnight in disguise, lay in hiding during day time in other countries so as not to be recognised and went about begging at night.

Ultimately he felt confident that his mind had matured sufficiently to be free from egoism. Then he decided to go to his native place and there went out begging in all the streets. As he was not recognised by anyone, he went one day to the palace itself. The watchman recognised him, made obeisance and informed the king about it, shivering with fear. The king came in a great hurry and requested him (Bhagiratha) to accept the kingdom back, but Bhagiratha did not agree. "Will you give me alms or not?", he asked. As there was no other alternative, they gave him alms and he went away highly pleased.

Subsequently he became the king of some other country for some reason and when the king of his own country passed away, he ruled that country also at the special request of the people. That story is given in detail in *Vasishtam*. The kingdom which earlier appeared to him to be a burden did not trouble him in the least after he attained *jnana*.

UNIVERSAL EQUALITY

In the course of a conversation about Sri Bhagavan's life in Madurai, Sri Bhagavan recalled, "If my aunt began preparing appalams, or the like, she would call me and ask me to put my hand on it first. She had great faith in me, because I used to do everything according to her wishes and never told lies. I had to tell only one lie and that was when I came here."

A devotee then said, "It means that for doing a great thing, sometimes a lie has to be told!"

Sri Bhagavan replied, "Yes. When it is for the welfare of the world and when the situation demands it, it has to be done. It cannot be helped. Where is the question of telling a lie? Some force makes one say so. So long as there is purpose there is need of action. When there is no purpose, we can avoid action in the same way as was done by the sage in the story of the sage and the hunter in Yoga Vasishtam.*"*

Full of curiosity the devotee asked, "What is that story?"

IN A FOREST, a sage sat motionless and in silence. His eyes however were open. A hunter hit a deer and as it was running away, he began pursuing it. When he saw the sage he stopped. The deer had run in front of the sage and hidden itself in a bush nearby. The hunter could not see it and so asked the sage "Swami, my deer has come running this way. Please tell me where exactly it has gone." The sage said he did not know. The hunter said, "It ran in front of you. Your eyes were open.

How could you say you do not know?", to which the sage replied, "Oh my friend! We are in the forest with universal equality. We do not have *ahankara*. Unless you have *ahankara*, you cannot do things in this world. That *ahankara* is the mind. That mind does all things. It also makes all the sense organs work. We certainly have no mind; it disappeared long ago. We do not have the three states – the states of waking, dream and deep sleep. We are always in the fourth or *turiya* state. In that state nothing is seen by us. That being so, what can we say about your deer?" Unable to understand what the sage was saying, the hunter went his way thinking they were all the words of a mad man.

ONE POINTEDNESS

A visitor wrote some questions in Tamil and presented them to Bhagavan. Bhagavan said, "He wants to know how to turn the mind from sense enjoyments and realise that bliss which is said to be so much above sense enjoyments. There is only one way – making the mind merge in That which is above sense enjoyments. As you concentrate on that, the sense attractions will fall of their own accord. Again he asked, 'When can I attain that bliss?' We are daily enjoying that bliss in sleep. We have not to attain bliss. We are bliss itself. Bliss is another name for us. It is our nature. Merging of the mind alone is necessary.

After a pause Bhagavan added, "The story of Indra and Ahalya in Yoga Vasishta *clearly illustrates how, by the force of the mind being merged in the one Reality, all other things will cease to affect one."*

AHALYA, THE WIFE of a king, falls in love with a rake called Indra. The matter reaches the king's ears and attains the magnitude of a great public scandal. The king then orders the couple to be put through various cruel tortures. But neither of them is affected by the tortures. Their faces do not even show a twitch of pain but are blissfully smiling at each other. The king, baffled by all this, asks them what the secret of their strength and resistance is. They say, "What! Don't you know? We are looking at each other, and so engrossed are we with each other, that our minds has no room for any other thoughts. So far as we are concerned, we two alone exist, each for the other, and nothing else exists. How then can we be affected by other things?" Such is the power of the merged mind.

THE *SIDDHAS'* LESSON

IN THE *VASISHTAM* it is stated that Rama, after his return from a pilgrimage, found that the whole world was full of misery and that bearing the body was itself a cause of misery. He, therefore left everything, even things like eating and drinking, and remained motionless. When Viswamitra asked Dasaratha to send Rama to guard his oblations ceremony (*yagna*), Dasaratha said that Rama was like a mad man and described some of the signs of his madness. On hearing them, Viswamitra said that he was very pleased to hear of those symptoms, that such madness did not come to many people and that he would like to see him and asked for him to be brought. Rama accordingly came, prostrated before all those present and sat down.

Viswamitra saw him and asked him the cause of his madness, and addressing Vasishta, said, "Please teach Rama the knowledge of the Self, the knowledge which Brahma taught you and me." Vasishta agreed to do so. While he was teaching, *siddhas* from all over came to listen to him and they thought to themselves, "Rama has gained so much knowledge at such a young age. How surprising! How great! What is the use of our living so long?"

GLOSSARY

A

Adi Saiva	:	One who bears the marks of Siva.
Adhyatma vidya	:	Knowledge of the *Atman* (Self).
Advaita	:	Non-duality. The doctrine that nothing exists apart from the Self, but everything is a form assumed by the Self.
Agamic	:	Relating to the *Agamas*, one of the Hindu scriptures.
Aham	:	I, embodied Self.
Ajnana	:	Ignorance.
Ajnani	:	One who has not realised the Self.
Akasvani	:	Voice coming from the sky.
Amba	:	An intimate name for the Divine Mother or a Goddess.
Amrita	:	Immortal.
Artha	:	Pertaining to material plane.
Ashram	:	Hermitage, establishment that grows up around a sage or *guru*.
Atma	:	The Spirit of Self.
Avadhuta	:	An ascetic who has given up everything.
Avatar	:	Incarnation, descent of God in a worldly form, divine manifestation.

B

Bhagavan	:	The term 'Bhagavan' is used for those few supreme sages who are recognised as being completely one with God.
Brahma	:	In the Hindu Trinity, the god of creation.
Brahmachari	:	A celibate.
Brahma Jnana	:	Knowledge (Realization of *Brahman*).
Brahman	:	The Supreme Being, the Absolute.
Brahmapuri	:	Heart, abode of *Brahma*.
Brahma Vidya	:	The knowledge of *Brahman*.
Brahmin	:	The Hindus were divided traditionally into four castes, of whom the *brahmins* were the highest being devoted to a life of spirituality and study.
Bhajan	:	Singing of God's praises, especially in chorus.
Bhakta	:	Devotee, one who approaches God through love and devotion.
Bhakti	:	Devotion to a personal God.

131

C

Chakra	:	A *Yogic* centre in the body.
Chinmudra	:	A hand-pose indicating illumination.
Chitakash	:	The space in the heart, *Brahman*.

D

Darsan	:	Lit: 'sight', seeing a holy man.
Dasi	:	Courtesan.
Devas	:	Celestial beings.
Devi	:	The Divine Mother or a Goddess.
Dharma	:	Harmony, harmonious life or action. Also a man's role in life, since what is harmonious conduct for one may not be so for another.
Dhyana	:	Meditation, contemplation.
Dikshitar	:	A priest.

G

Ganapathi	:	The eldest son of Siva, whose head is that of an elephant.
Gandharvas	:	Semi divine beings expert in dance and singing.
Ganesh (Ganesa)	:	A name for *Ganapathi*.
Gayathri	:	A well-known *Vedic mantra*.
Gowri (Gouri)	:	A name for *Parvati*, the wife of *Siva*.
Guru	:	Spiritual guide or master.

H

Hara	:	A name for *Siva*
Harikatha	:	A religious discourse interspersed with devotional songs.

I

Iswara (Isvara)	:	Personal God, the Supreme Being in His aspect of the Lord of the World. An intimate reference to God.

J

Jagrat	:	Waking state.
Japa	:	Repetition of a sacred word, syllable or name of God.
Jivanmukti	:	Liberated while one is alive.

132

Jnani	:	One who is the repository of *jnana*, (knowledge), A Self-realised sage.

K

Kailas	:	A mountain in the Himalayas reputed to be the abode of Lord *Siva*.
Kalpa	:	The end of a period in time.
Karma	:	Action, deeds. The destiny that a person makes for himself by the law of cause and effect.
Karnam	:	One who keeps accounts on landed property.
Kolaru Padikam	:	A hymn in praise of Lord Siva explaining that the planets are powerless and can do no harm to the devotee if only the Lord condescends to bless him.
Kowpeenam (Kaupeenam)	:	Loin cloth.

L

Linga	:	A symbol representing *Siva* or the Absolute. Lit: 'that in which all beings are absorbed.'

M

Mahadeva	:	A name for *Siva*.
Maharshi	:	Great Seer, Great *Rishi*.
Mahatma	:	Enlightened person.
Mahendra	:	A name for *Siva*.
Maheswara	:	A name for *Siva*.
Mantra	:	Sacred syllables, through repetition of which one attains perfection.
Marga	:	Mode of approach in the spiritual quest.
Mauna (Mouna)	:	Silence.
Maya	:	Illusion; the power inherent in Brahman by which it manifests the world.
Moksha	:	Liberation, spiritual freedom.
Mount Meru	:	The mountain which, in Hindu mythology is the spiritual centre of the universe.
Mutt (Math)	:	A monastery where mendicants live

N

Nayana diksha	:	Initiation by sight.

P

Parameswara	:	A name for *Siva*.
Parvati	:	In Hindu mythology the consort of *Siva*.
Prakriti	:	Nature, *Maya*.
Pranayama	:	Regulation or control of breath.
Prarabdha	:	The part of one's *karma* which is to be worked out in this life.
Periapuranam	:	An ancient Tamil work depicting the lives of 63 *Saivite* Saints.

R

Rama	:	An incarnation of *Vishnu*.
Ramayana	:	An Indian epic depicting the life of *Rama*.
Rati	:	In Hindu Mythology the wife of Cupid.
Rishi (Rshi)	:	Sage, Seer.
Rudraksha	:	Lit. Siva's eyes. Beads used for *Japa*.

S

Sadhaka	:	A spiritual aspirant, a seeker.
Sadhana	:	Method of spiritual practice.
Sadhu	:	Ascetic. One who has renounced home.
Saivite	:	Worshipper of Lord *Siva*.
Samadhi	:	Absorption in the Spirit or Self, with or without trance and suspension of the human faculties.
Sama Veda	:	One of the *Vedas*.
Sambhu	:	A name of *Siva, Siva* as the bounteous.
Sannyasa	:	Asceticism, the fourth stage of life.
Sannyasi	:	An ascetic, one who has renounced home, property, caste and all attachments in the spiritual quest.
Sastra	:	Any branch of knowledge or science.
Sati	:	Self-immolation by a wife on the funeral-pyre of her husband.
Siddha Purusha	:	A sage possessing supernatural powers.
Siddhi	:	Supernatural power, attainment.
Sita	:	In Hindu Mythology the wife of *Rama*.
Siva	:	Lord of the Universe, in the Hindu Trinity, the god of destruction.
Siva Bhakti Vilasam	:	Collection of stories on *Siva*.
Siva Lingam	:	The symbol of *Siva* which is an object of worship.

Srutis	:	Scriptural texts passed on by the verbal medium.
Subrahmanya	:	In Hindu Mythology the second son of *Siva*.
Sushupti	:	Dreamless sleep.
Swapna	:	Dream.
Swarupa	:	Nature, real form, self.

T

Tapas	:	Penance or austerities.
Tapasvini	:	A female who performs *tapas*.
Tapasaya	:	Intense Spiritual discipline.
Tapo Brashta	:	One who has fallen from his *tapas*.
Tirtha	:	Sacred water.
Turiya	:	The Fourth state beyond waking, dreaming and sleeping.

U

Upadesa	:	Spiritual instruction.

V

Van Thondan	:	The name for Sundaramurthy Nayanar, one of the four principal *Saivite* saints.
Vasanas	:	Latencies or tendencies inherent in man.
Vedas	:	The earliest Hindu scriptures, revealed to the ancient *Rishis*.
Venba	:	A type of verse in Tamil.
Vichara	:	Enquiry.
Vichara Marga	:	The spiritual path of enquiry.
Vishnu	:	Supreme Lord. In the Hindu Trinity, the god of preservation.

Y

Yoga	:	Lit. Union (with the Supreme Being).
Yagna	:	Ritualistic sacrifice.
Yogi	:	One who follows or has mastered the path of Yoga (path of union).

APPENDIX

Important Events in Sri Bhagavan's Life

1879 December 30, Monday – corresponding to 16, *Margali* of Tamil Year *Pramadi* – Star *Punarvasu* – *Ardra Darshan* Day – Born at 1 a.m. at Tiruchuli (*'Sri Sundara Mandiram'*).

1891 Moves to Dindigul, after completing elementary education at Tiruchuli.

1892 February 18: Death of father, Sundaram Iyer. Moves to Madurai. Studies at Scott's Middle School and American Mission High School.

1895 November: Hears of 'Arunachala' mentioned to him by an elderly relative.

1896 (about middle of July): 'Death Experience' at Madurai ending in complete and permanent Realisation of the Self (*'Sri Ramana Mandiram'*).

August 29, Saturday: Leaves Madurai for Arunachala.

September 1 – Tuesday: Arrives in Arunachala – Stays in the Temple premises within the Thousand-pillared Hall, beneath the *Illupai* Tree, in *Pathala Linga* (underground cellar), sometimes in the *Gopuram*.

1897 Moves to Gurumurtam in the outskirts of the town (early in the year).

Stays in the shrine and the adjoining Mango grove.

1898 May: Uncle Nelliappa Iyer visits Bhagavan at Mango grove.

September: Moves to Pavalakkunru.

December: Mother Alagammal visits Bhagavan at Pavalakkunru.

1899 February: Moves to the Hill, Arunachala. Stays in various caves up the Hill, but mostly in Virupaksha Cave, using Mango Tree Cave as summer residence.

1900 Replies to questions put by Gambiram Seshayya, at Virupaksha Cave.

1902 *(The above published as Self-enquiry)*

1902 Answers to questions asked by Sivaprakasam Pillai (*Who am I?*)

1905 Moves to Pachaiamman Koil for six months during the plague epidemic – returns to the Hill.

1907 November 18: Momentous meeting between Bhagavan and Kavyakanta Ganapati Muni. Bhagavan imparts *upadesa* to Muni.

1908 (January to March): Stays at Pachaiamman Koil (with Ganapati Muni and others) and again goes back to Virupaksha Cave.

Translates into Tamil prose Adi Sankara's *Viveka Chudamanai* and *Drik Drisya Viveka*.

1911 November: F.H. Humphreys, the first Westerner, meets Bhagavan.

1912 Second death experience at Tortoise Rock in the presence of Vasudeva Sastry and others.

1914 Offers prayers (songs) to Arunachala for Mother's recovery from illness.

1915 The *Song of the Pappadum* written for the sake of mother. The following were also written during Virupaksha days:

Arunachala Aksharamanamalai, *Arunachala Padikam*, *Arunachala Ashtakam*, Translation of *Devi Kalottara*, Translation of Adi Sankara's *Hymn to Dakshinamurti*, *Guru Stuti* and *Hastamalaka Stotra*.

1916 Moves to Skandashram.

1917 Composes *Arunachala Pancharatnam* in Sanskrit.

Mother settles at Skandashram. *Sri Ramana Gita* in Sanskrit written by Ganapati Muni.

1922 May 19, Friday: Mother's *Maha Samadhi*.

Middle of December: Moves to the present site of *Sri Ramanasramam*.

1927 Composes *Upadesa Sara* in Tamil, Telugu, Sanskrit and Malayalam.

April 24: Composes *Atma Vidya* (Self Knowledge).

1928 Composes *Ulladu Narpadu* (Forty Verses on Reality) in Tamil and Malayalam (*Sat Darshanam*).

1930 *Sat Darshanam* in Sanskrit (translated from Tamil by Ganapati Muni).

1933 Translated into Tamil the *Agama: Sarvajnanotharam – Atma Sakshatkara*.

1939 September 1, Thursday: Foundation laid by Bhagavan for the Matrubhuteswara Temple.

1940 Selects 42 verses from *The Bhagavad Gita* (now entitled The Song Celestial) and translates them into Tamil and Malayalam.

1947 February: Composes *Ekatma Panchakam* (Five Verses on the Self) in Telugu and Tamil.

1948 June 18: Cow Lakhsmi attains *Nirvana*.

Translates into Tamil *Atma Bodha* of Adi Sankara.

1949 March 17, Thursday – *Kumbabhishekam* of Matrubhuteswara Temple in the presence of Bhagavan.

1950 April 14, Friday: *Brahma Nirvana* of Bhagavan at 8-47 p.m. At that moment a shooting star, vividly luminous, coming from the South (the present *Nirvana* Room) and moving slowly northward across the sky and disappearing behind the peak of Arunachala was observed by many in various parts of India.

Sri Ramanarpanamasthu